Shifting the Dials

To Quinn and to Kit: to show that with love, support and creativity, the wildest dreams are within reach.

And to Nick: for giving me that love and support (I'm taking credit for the creativity!). Love you!

Shifting the Dials

A New Approach for Success in Work and Life

Rebecca Anderton-Davies

First published in Great Britain in 2023 by Yellow Kite
An imprint of Hodder & Stoughton
An Hachette UK company

1

A CIP catalogue record for this title is available from the British Library

Trade Paperback ISBN 978 1 399 70373 4
eBook ISBN 978 1 399 70374 1

Typeset in Celeste by Hewer Text UK Ltd, Edinburgh
Printed and bound in Great Britain by Clays Ltd, Elcograf S.p.A.

Hodder & Stoughton policy is to use papers that are natural, renewable
and recyclable products and made from wood grown in sustainable
forests. The logging and manufacturing processes are expected to
conform to the environmental regulations of the country of origin.

Yellow Kite
Hodder & Stoughton Ltd
Carmelite House
50 Victoria Embankment
London EC4Y 0DZ

www.yellowkitebooks.co.uk

CONTENTS

INTRODUCTION

_____

HOW CAN YOU have a career _and_ a life you love, in a world which still isn't set up for you to do either of those things with ease?

If I was being generous, I'd say this was a conundrum.

If I was being direct, I'd say this was bullshit.

If I was being precise, I'd say there are three completely different but equally wrong answers to this very real problem.

The first bullshit answer is that everything will be fine and dandy if you magically find 'work–life balance'. Because work–life balance is impossible. Straight up. As is anything static in the dynamic and ever-changing thing we call time. It is a two-dimensional approach for a four-dimensional world.

It's also not even _preferable_. Even if you could 'get' that 'balance', it would be a poisoned chalice. The categories of 'life' and 'work' are woefully insufficient – thinking about the span of decades ahead of us and the days we are living right now in this binary fashion sets us up for disappointment and unmet expectations from the off.

On top of that, living in these human bodies in this current culture means that frequently we simply have to be more 'all-in' than any sense of 'balance' allows us. Having a baby, going for a big promotion, caring for an ill loved one, doing a degree or an internship, moving house, doing the 'big job' . . . take your pick: life happens in a series of opportunities, challenges and seasons, each of which requires wildly different allocations of our time and energy to wildly different priorities. And this happens again and again over the hopefully wide spans of our lifetimes.

Which all makes the concept of 'work–life balance' a useless, and frankly toxic, mental model. Because that is what it is meant to be, right? A quick framework, a speedy rule of thumb for operating. One that is meant to help us find a sense of fulfilment in the rare and precious years we get to spend on this rare and precious earth, but which in fact does the opposite.

Yet despite its unhelpfulness, we cannot escape it. Women in leadership positions or who are living their life in any public way at all get asked it repeatedly. Crikey, how many of us ask it of ourselves it in the quiet of the early morning hours, brain whirring, doubts flaring. Questioning why everyone else has cracked this thing that we are failing at. Because it's *everywhere* in our culture. This book, I hope, is a final nail in work–life balance's well-deserved and long-overdue coffin.

The second bullshit answer is to 'lean in'. Saying this isn't especially new some 10 years after Sheryl Sandburg's book espoused us to do just that. Try harder, assert better, demand more, then success will follow. The backlash to this, rightly, spoke to the truth that it was not – is not – that simple. The message did not take account of the systemic barriers that women, and especially women of colour, Black women and those who are intersectional in anyway, face. But this point is even more pertinent right now – in a (please) post-COVID world. Never have we had a starker illustration of the depth of structural injustice some face than the two years of the COVID-19 pandemic.

Women made up 39 per cent of global employment but accounted for 54 per cent of overall job losses during the pandemic.[1] In the UK, mothers were 23 per cent more likely than fathers to have lost their jobs (temporarily or permanently) during the first COVID lockdown. In families where the father lost his job while the mother kept hers, men and women still split housework and childcare responsibilities equally. In all other types of households, mothers spent substantially more time on domestic responsibilities.[2] In Britain, a quarter of families are headed by a single parent, more than 90 per cent of whom are women.[3] So who picked up the slack when schools closed?

And, unsurprisingly but tragically, the reality only gets worse for Black women and women of colour, all of whom have been acutely affected by pre-existing inequalities across a huge range of areas, including health, employment and access to government support.[4] One last illustration: in the US, the employment-to-population ratio of Black women in their prime working years in 2021 was still 3.4 percentage points below the rate it was one year before the pandemic began, compared with 2.3 percentage points for all other women and 1.9 percentage points for white women. There are currently roughly 257,700 fewer employed prime-age Black women in the US than a year before the pandemic, when if you account for population growth, there should be over 312,500 *more*.[5]

Trying harder did not, will not, solve this. Leaning in isn't fixing the gender pay gap, the even larger racial gender pay gap, the lack of flexible working or affordable childcare, the mismatched allocation of caring and domestic responsibilities on women, the motherhood penalty or the everyday prejudice and discrimination that is still so prevalent.

So what are we meant to do? We can't do it all by ourselves. The system isn't doing it for us – quite the opposite. And, importantly, **there is no magic 'refuse to participate' button. We are here. In this world. In this time. In this system. This is the only chance we get.** The only chance to live, to work, to thrive. To adventure, to laugh, to cry, to parent, to love, to discover, to think, to build, to fix, to do whatever it is we want.

Which brings me to the third bullshit answer: making your lifestyle your work. We are spun a lie by those who implore us to nakedly 'follow our passions' and that if we 'do what we love' then we'll never work a day in our lives. If only it were that simple. If only. Many people do not have easily monetisable passions, or just want to keep them protected from the complications of earning a living from them. None of us is one thing alone, and we don't have to be the one thing that gets us paid.

The post-'lean in' era saw the rise of two phenomena, the first amplified by the second: the almost deification of all things entrepreneurial, and the explosion of social media. In the context of the need to escape the confines of the old, intractable workplace structures, this of course made perfect sense. Building your own small or empire-like business and bringing the world along for the ride meant you were setting your own rules, at last. You could create a unicorn while barely out of school, your kitchen-table business could find a bigger audience, or you could get paid to go on holiday or wear nice clothes or try on make-up or even do yoga poses. <Insert hair flick here.>

Except, what is more relentless and critical and unforgiving: a boss or an algorithm or a customer or an investor? I've done the first three and I can tell you which I prefer. My point isn't that building your own business or working in social media is a wrong or bad option. But it isn't the easy option. And anyone who suggests it is, including the 'follow your dreams' crew, is being dishonest about the myriad of challenges that lie ahead on those paths.

The nugget of truth here is that there are no easy options. There are only numerous different trades – gives and takes – each of us must make. And it is only possible to select the ones that are best, or at a minimum least worst, for each of us if we a) are honest about them in the first place and b) know what is uniquely important to us as individuals. *This* is how it becomes possible to live with some sense of ease. It isn't about things being easy, **it's about getting enough control and building enough resilience into your life that you get to choose the struggles that suit *you* best.** Which is why the second half of this book is dedicated to discussing many of these trades: quitting, fulfilment, passions, hobbies, flexibility, money and impact.

My route to more ease has been to choose an unconventional way of walking a conventional path. The 'traditional', or maybe even extreme, corporate career, as a woman and mother. I am some 18 years into a career in investment banking – interning and temping my way through university, then embarking on a full-time career upon graduation, first in operations (processing trades), then seven years as a currency sales-trader (shouting 'buy buy buy' into old-school phone handsets). Then nine as a senior relationship manager (looking after big complicated clients across the entire bank's business). And, as of very recently, embarking on a new phase of my career building and running a new exchange-traded fund launching service within the bank. At the same time, I have been discovering, maintaining and sharing a passion for yoga and, it turns out, writing, quite publicly on social media and on these pages. It has involved a long-standing marriage, birthing two gorgeous boys and navigating shared parental leave, co-parenting and dual careering with my husband too.

I tell you this as not many people get to write books like this. On careers and on life, that is. The people we normally get to hear from on the career front are the founders, the C-suiters, the unicorners. They are the multi-multi-millionaires who have cracked the secrets of success, those who have (seemingly) 'won' the game of life and want to tell us how to follow in their footsteps.

Or they are the creatives and activists. The writers and media people, the ones who have cultivated a platform and now use it, professionally. The ones who do not do the 9–5s or, more accurately, the 8–6s or 7–7s. Maybe they did for a few years. Then they 'escaped'. And now they can tell us we can too.

And I *love* books by them all, ordering the next ones on Amazon even as the stack of unread books grows higher and more unstable on my bedside table. Recommending them to friends, handing them out to colleagues, jotting down notes as I inhale a chapter or two on the train to work.

But I am none of those people. And have no plans to be.

It is a truly strange mix of events which got me here. There was a bike accident involving a white van. There was, is, an unplanned career in investment banking that continues at a level I am proud of, but is far, far away from reaching anything C-suite. There were hours of (badly) practising yoga, being gently pestered by two very cute cats, to recover from the accident. There was a lovely but inexplicable growth of Instagram 'followers' along for the ride. There was a firstly self-published book on yoga self-practice which stumbled out of its not-worth-publishing niche only because of the brutal realities of a global pandemic and worldwide lockdowns.

None of this screams 'read my book about life and work'!

Except that's kind of the point.

Certain kinds of content and certain kinds of people and certain kinds of jobs 'work' in the media, be that social or traditional, getting book deals or TikTok followers. This is not a judgement. It is a simple statement of fact. I am not naive about why my yoga account took off on Instagram in the way it did; it's not hard to imagine it doing very differently if my skin was a different shade or my body a different size. Similarly, it is incredibly difficult to 'do' social media from a corporate seat at all (Compliance departments rejoice!), forget about doing it *justice*. Confidentiality being a huge piece of it, as well as the fact that meetings aren't the most engaging content for socials, even if the topics, and more importantly the processes, pace, people, perks and pay packets, may be.

This, of course, is why we get to hear from the CEOs: they can set the rules (and hire a nice ghostwriter to pitch their message). Yet, in the UK alone, there are over 10 million people employed by large corporations. That is nearly 40 per cent of the entire private sector employment.[6] There may be a few thousand CEOs in there, but there are thousands of times more people in the middle somewhere carving paths and trying to find the right trades too.

We need to hear from *more* people on these topics. We need *more* discussion of the various trades in various walks of life. Not only is there space for everyone, but the discussion gets richer the more voices are a part of it. I want to hear from those who have completed the game (hello billionaires and CEOs) *and* those who have eschewed the game as we used to know it (hello influencers and digital nomads) *and* those who want to change the rules of the game (hello activists). And then *more* from those in the different places entirely. Yes, maybe a few more mid-level corporate types.

My experience as one of those, by definition, cannot be totally inclusive or representative. I'm a middle-class white woman raised in a wealthy country by a military father and a teacher mother. The privilege of my work in an incredibly well-paid industry has afforded me a level of security and, frankly, comfort that is not available to all (money is a subject we will spend an entire chapter on later in the book). Being a woman in a male-dominated industry and a patriarchal society has given me some experience of structural challenges and disadvantages. Yet it does not compare to what people of colour or those who are intersectional in any way must face, both at work and in society at large. I get to 'check my privilege' here on this page, rather than try to navigate a reality which has Black women on a 108-year long journey, at current rates of progress, to equal pay. Or 202 years for Hispanic women. Compared to 'just' 33 for white women versus white men.[7]

Any 'solution' which ignores all these realities is no solution at all. Nor is one which is explicit about them but only focuses on what needs to change.

We need to live, to thrive. Right here. Right now. In this world.

We need a mental model – a framework – that helps everyone, but women especially, to find more joy and more fulfilment and more of whatever it is they want from life. One that is easily changeable, speaks honestly about the world *and* gives useful tools to operate in it as it is, not as we wish it to be. So that we might have the energy, vision, and strength to one day make it precisely that: more as we wish it to be.

As with all things in life, there are very few universal right answers – there are only the right answers for each of us in that moment, and many, many trades to make along the way. The clearer we each can be about what we want and do not want, what we have and do not have, what we can and cannot do, and what is and is not possible, the more likely we are to make decisions that work for us – in the great moments of life and in the awful ones, because all our lives will be full of both.

I cannot promise that this book is going to change the world. What I can promise, however, is a framework that is just as short as 'work–life balance', but a hell of a lot less useless and toxic. One that, I hope, can be utilised in many walks of life, for many different component parts of life and many different ways of allocating energy to them. One that helps you work out which trades are right for you, and then supports you to live with them. To find some ease in a world which is rarely easy.

This framework is 'The Dials'.

The Dials is a flexible, open, empowering approach to working life – not work and life as separate entities, but as a series of constantly evolving and coexisting components, reflective of an honest assessment of your values, goals and priorities. The Dials is a method that encourages you to expand your notions of both 'life' and 'work', and then fashion a sustainable, nourishing and, most of all, realistic way of knitting all those many pieces of a rich and varied existence together – one which changes over time but works for today *and* for the long term.

Instead of a static, binary impossibility, The Dials is a dynamic tool, made up of four parts: dashboard, dials, levels, resilience. It is a snapshot of current times and a process to be worked through; it is a reflection of where you are at in this moment, and a series of steps you can revisit in a discrete and/or continuous way from here on out.

We are going to go through each step in depth over the coming chapters. I'm going to make the case for why every piece is an essential one, explain how it works and how to best approach it, and share stories and examples which further illustrate and give guidance on the practical how-tos. Throughout the book, there will be questions and prompts to help you start thinking about what The Dials will look like for you.

We will sketch out each section of your Dials as we travel through this first half of the book. In the second half, we are going to spend some time on topics that your Dials all relate to:

quitting, how a life helps rather than hinders a career, career fulfilment, trades in life and work, money and impact. It is my hope that, by the end of the book, you will be able to bring all of this together to finalise your personal Dials framework.

So, jot down notes in the margins as you go, fill in the blank spaces as you get to them, highlight passages that you want to stay with you, and feel free to disagree with me along the way too. This will all form the basis of *your* framework, *your* dials. Any notes you make along the way, or thoughts that begin to coalesce, need not be perfect or even fully formed. The idea is that they will develop as we travel through the rest of the book, together.

I will be sharing many of my personal stories in these pages. Not because you should do what I have done – not at all – but because they further illuminate an example of using The Dials framework and the very real questions that arise when we try to work out what having a successful approach to work and to life looks like for us. These stories, I hope, will be illustrative, even if they are not – indeed, cannot be – representative. You will also see many quotes, comments and stories from a range of different people working through The Dials framework, giving you further examples of how The Dials can help clarify thinking, litmus-test choices and enable the expression of priorities in the real world. You will see quotes, stories and thoughts from different people throughout the book: these are based on numerous real interviews, but mostly created here as composites and with identifying details tweaked, all to represent key themes that came up in those conversations repeatedly. Again, they won't be entirely representative, but I hope they are helpful. And that, one day, I will be able to hear from you and other readers about your own Dials.

I have not reached any level of perfection or eliminated all difficulty from my own life. I *definitely* do not have the perfect answers of how to do *your* life right. This isn't a book about how to do things my way. What this is is a book about how to do things *your* way, in *our* world. Your priorities, your path. Your set of guiding principles with which to navigate the choppy waters of life.

Because it happens, right – #life – in all its messy and complex glory. It can be really, really hard. And really, really wonderful.

I know that I have a set of guiding principles and a practical mental model that I can turn to whatever piece of good or bad news or exciting or difficult set of choices come barrelling at me next. And I want you to have that too.

Part 1

THE DIALS

Chapter 1

THE ALTERNATIVE TO WORK–LIFE BALANCE

'IT IS LITERALLY ridiculous to think that.'

I didn't even know how to respond at this point.

She continued: 'Look, there are so many problems with what you are telling me. Let's start with your marriage.'

I was now deeply regretting my decision to persuade my husband to do this coaching call with me, on the coach's insistence. At least if he hadn't heard any of this, I could brush it under the proverbial carpet. Instead, I could feel him start to simmer, disbelief and offence oozing out of every pore. He never understood my admiration of this woman in the first place. And here she was trashing our entire life plan. Maybe even our entire life.

'You are telling me you want all these kids and both of you want to work, but that he will step back from work after the first. That is totally unrealistic.'

She systematically tore through us as individuals, us as a couple and the multi-year dream-slash-plan that I had sketched out for her, and that I had already spent the years of my twenties quite literally pouring my blood, sweat and tears into.

She told us there was no way I would want to go back to work six months after having a baby. And that, as I had more, I would want to give up work entirely. She told us that my husband would need to quit his current career path and pivot radically to become the breadwinner. That if he didn't, our family would never be happy, that I would never be happy. She told us that there was no way the best-in-class investment bank I worked for would support the nascent passion I was cultivating in yoga and sharing on Instagram, and that my career would stall.

We hung up the phone. My husband and I turned to face each other.

A pause. Fish mouths, gasping silently for air, reaching for words. And, after a moment, we laughed. Haltingly at first – more out of disbelief, and then out of an early conviction that she was the one who had no sense of what was realistic.

Here she was, this career coach, who had raised her family on the fruits of professionally giving advice and public speaking.

How could anyone think that marriages with kids would only work with male breadwinners? How could this professional think that corporates were so out of touch that they would punish their high performers for being high performers in their lives outside of work? How could she not understand how much fulfilment I got from my career? How could she not see, not hear, that our marriage is truly equal?

It was late 2017. I was fresh off the disappointment of not having made a big promotion at work and facing a two-year wait to go for it again. And, unbeknown to me at that point, a handful of weeks pregnant with our first child. I was also at one of those wobble points, that anyone more than a few years into a big career will know all too well. Doubts had crept in, and maybe she was right. Maybe we were wrong. Maybe our life, my life, was never going to work.

UNPICKING WORK–LIFE BALANCE

It's a strange thing, balance. Strictly speaking it's an equilibrium – a lack of movement, where the net force in all directions, by definition, is zero. At least, that is what the physicists agree on.

Yet, most of us would say that balance is something we are striving for. Trying, searching, hustling for. Something we put huge amounts of effort in to find. And, if we do, even for just the briefest of moments, we try even harder to keep it.

But when the first condition of equilibrium is that there is absolutely no net force present, it seems incongruous that we think putting more effort in will help us. Yet this is precisely what we do when it comes to work–life balance. Because it is this prized ideal – something we are told we should have, should want.

I'm sure I had already soaked up the cultural meaning and supposed importance of all things work–life balance by the time I hit my twenties. But the first conscious encounter I had with it was in the months heading into my first real job after university.

I got that job in late 2006 – on my mother's birthday to be precise. It's wild that I remember those little details so clearly, all these years later. I think because I had an inkling then, and as I know now, that I'd been lucky enough to hit a railroad switch that shunted me onto an entirely different life track. I called my mum, wishing her a happy birthday, and, crying into the mirror as we spoke, told her that I'd been offered a place on the so-called 'grad scheme' on the trading floor at a large Swiss investment bank.

I was in my final year at university and had been variously interning and temping at an even larger American investment bank since the summer after I left school. So, it wasn't some huge surprise. But it was a big deal, at least in our small world. No one we knew then had worked in a career like this. I had stumbled into that first internship courtesy of a friend at school.

He had been told about it by the careers-counsellor-slash-history-teacher, yet he thought it was more up my street than his; knowing my hodgepodge of waitressing, checkout and shelf-stacking jobs which were already doing their bit to pay for the incoming degree costs, and my general ambition to do 'something in business'.

The internship and temp jobs were in 'operations', aka 'the back office'. This is where trades are processed, payments sent and the other less glamorous but totally necessary mechanics behind the buying-and-selling of financial instruments happen. I didn't love the work, which mainly involved repetitive tasks such as checking the basic time/date/amount/account details against the equivalent entries from other banks, but it was infinitely more pleasant even than the very best days at all my previous jobs. I got to dress up smartly rather than wear an ill-fitting polyester uniform. I had my own desk, surrounded by chatty colleagues, rather than spending countless hours on my feet dodging irate chefs and drunk customers. I did not have to spend the dark weeks of one particularly grim Christmas holiday on night shifts in my local supermarket stacking cheese in a freezing chiller aisle, sleeping for a few hours then dashing to do the lunchtime shift waitressing at a local pub.

Over the three years of my degree, I spent some 12 months interning or temping, and had tried and failed to get a classic (read: mergers and acquisitions) investment banking internship in that middle summer. So, applying for grad schemes felt like it was my only remaining shot. I applied for positions at 20 different banks, was interviewed for five and was offered that single job.

So yes, it felt like a big deal.

I spent the next 10 months before the job officially started buzzing with excitement, and lots of relief. I relished answering the questions that every 'grown-up' (friends' parents, lecturers, neighbours) asks a final-year university student: what are you doing next, do you have a job?

I did! And when I excitedly shared my news, all people wanted to ask me about was ... you guessed it ... work–life balance.

Again and again as I shared my news, an eyebrow would creep up, a doubt would sneak out: 'Oh wow, that's exciting, better get prepared for no sleep and no life for the next few years!'; 'Investment banking you say ... Isn't that where work–life balance is impossible?'; 'Ah, so you're writing off your twenties then.'

At the time, I shook most of it off, confused as to why people seemed so obsessed about a singular decision being either definitive, or indeed wrong, at this early stage of my life. After all, I was 21 years old. Still at university. On the threshold of a new and exciting stage of life, and potentially a great career. Looking ahead at a decade, at least, of few responsibilities, just lots of adventures and learning and the building of a foundation of my adult life.

Now I look back even more bewildered. Why did work–life balance matter so much? Why did everyone seem to care about something that by its very definition is a stasis – about lack of movement, a lack of force, a lack of momentum – when I was at the precise moment in my life that was surely meant to be about moving forward?

My wild guess/informed opinion/late-night ranting stream of consciousness response to this is two-fold. Firstly, of course, people were reacting to the stories they had heard about the industry: the 100-hour working weeks, the sleeping under desks and the like. But it's not like there aren't lots of people going into jobs, careers, that will entail long hours and intense pressure:

the world of finance, yes, but also lots and lots of other sectors – medicine, law and tech being some obvious examples. But some 15+ years later I have seen for real just how many hours a week teachers put in or how all-in jobs in the fashion industry can be.

Now I realise that people weren't reacting to *what* I was telling them, but what *I* was telling them. The person who was telling them was female. This whole work–life balance thing that people were so intent on reminding me as I headed out on the early days of my career wasn't related to concerns that were unique to *me* or my situation. It wasn't about banking or that they thought *Rebecca* needed more life than the next person. They were about the things that were generically me: that I was female. And there is something more *woman* about work–life balance.

It's not that women care more about having work–life balance than men – the data shows that men are much more likely to say that they don't spend enough time with their kids, largely due to work obligations.[1] It is that they are *expected* to care more about it, so get questioned accordingly.

There is a wonderful/awful story told by Hollywood actress Jennifer Garner, once married to fellow actor Ben Affleck, about how they compared notes on the questions they were asked during a day of interviews on a press junket. This is Garner: 'I told him every single person who interviewed me – and I mean every single one . . . asked me: "How do you balance work and family?"' She then recounted how her (then) husband explained that the only question he got asked consistently was about the breasts of the co-star in the movie he was doing the press for and how, in fact, not a single interviewer had asked him about how he combined his career with his family life, despite them doing the same job, and raising the same three kids together.[2]

The reason not one journalist asked Ben Affleck about who was looking after his kids while he ogled the breasts of his co-star was because no one expected him to be responsible for them, even though the data again shows that men care just as much about all these things as women: in surveys through the COVID-19 crisis, similar proportions of men and women found it more difficult to maintain a healthy work–life balance and preferred working from home because it meant a better work–life balance. [3,4]

'Balance' is not achievable

It would be easy for me now to say that work–life balance sucks because it is so misogynist and patriarchal, and be done with it. And while these issues are both very real and highly problematic, not least because they remove options from and limit the happiness of men too, the fundamental problem is that work–life balance fails to help any of us with the practicalities of living while working, or working while living, or balancing work and life, or whatever the hell we are meant to do day after day, year after year as adults in modern society. And this, surely, is the point.

It is meant to be a mental model: a framework which both helps us understand the world, and then, crucially, make decisions and solve problems. This is what everyone was getting at when they quizzed me about how I was going to manage as I became an investment banker aged just 21. Or why journalists pressed the female movie star rather than the male movie star about working while parenting.

The mental model of work–life balance starts with a binary: work versus life, one or the other, on–off, yes–no, start–stop. Yet is this at all how work and life, forgive me, work? The answer is, of course not. The reality we are facing is that, without paid work, it is very hard to live any kind of life. Housing, food, clothing: these things cost money. The flip side being that if we can't afford to feed or clothe ourselves, there isn't going to be a lot of productive work happening either.

The way this model is presented to us suggests that 'balance' between work and life is not only optimal, but attainable. That there is a perfect number of hours to spend at work and not-at-work to be happy, if you just keep searching, keep trying, keep . . . going. But that is not a choice that is available to anyone but the smallest percentage of humans. For the rest of us, it is instead a question of managing it all *together*.

Marc

I haven't got back on an even keel after the pandemic. Working out how work is meant to work and how family is meant to work, forget about together, has me at the limit. It's not sustainable.

And there is another problem here: who decided that all things 'life' get crammed into one category – work versus everything else? From the mundane but necessary sleeping and eating and washing, to the no less important elements of life like friendship, love, hobbies, moving your body, family, kids, seeing the world, inhaling art and music and culture, or just the entire latest hit series on Netflix in a single sitting. That this is all meant to sit in one neat category, totally opposed to anything that pays us, must surely be a miscategorisation of epic proportions.

This is obvious, of course, but worth specifically pointing out. Because categorising life as a simple, discrete bucket at one moment is bad enough. But if this is your starting point, then you are heading down a road which compounds that mistake over time.

Life isn't a single thing in a single moment, ever. Forget about over a *lifetime*.

What we need or want or can do with the non-work portion of our existence in our twenties, or thirties, or sixties is going to look massively different. The amount of socialising happening over the first few months of maternity leave is going to look like another planet versus the summer months in your late twenties or early thirties when every person in your friendship group seems to be getting married. The week of moving house, or going on holiday, or spent at the bedside of a sick family member will look, and of course feel, incomparably different.

But this is all life. And, importantly, not just the individual experiences or choices, but the *variation over time*. And the emphasis on trying to optimise it in opposition to work, in balance to work, as static, gets so far away from the very things that make life, well, worth living. We'll return to this idea later because it is so important.

Time is not neutral

This focus on how we each allocate time also distracts us from another important truth: time is not neutral. The simple number of hours or years allocated to a particular pursuit can consume a vastly different amount of physical or emotional energy. We each have limited amounts of these to start with, so the allocation of that scare resource should be something we explicitly think about. After all, certain activities are going to have a replenishing effect on those stores, while others will be a permanent drain.

A simplistic example of this would be to compare a workday at a job you hate versus one you love, or a day full of the subjects you sucked at during school versus those in which you excelled. Chances are you bounded home from the latter, full of stories about your day and ready to get stuck into whatever was ahead that evening. It's a better person than me who can come home from a bad day and not inhale the tub of ice cream from the freezer or who is able to clear their mind enough for a perfect night's sleep. And research confirms this correlation: people with a higher psychological well-being are more likely to exercise and eat well, as well as to sleep better – all things that themselves turn back into more energy to go out and do that next good day even better.[5,6] Or indeed, get through tomorrow's potentially hard day – a topic we will revisit in more depth in the following chapters.

What this expending of energy is bringing you is even more important to consider. Those hours or years of time can get you a step further away from or several steps closer to your goals and a version of life you will find deeply fulfilling.

Are you balancing the books of work versus life on an hours basis, keeping your energy stores replenished and, at best, just treading water? Or are work and life seemingly hugely imbalanced, yet you are in one of those exact moments you have been aiming for all along? Wouldn't that be the moment to pause, to wallow deliciously in that experience, to drink it in and savour it? Dare I say to *live* it rather than work/live it, or indeed balance it? Again, we are going to get into real-world examples of all of this throughout the book.

The language we use matters

Sure, 'work–life balance' is three short words, just 15 letters long. Maybe it is unreasonable to expect it to encompass everything that is important. Perhaps. Maybe I'm straw-manning this a little. But something keeps bringing me back to the stories I shared at the start of this chapter, and the hundreds, thousands more I know we could all share of the same ilk. There is an almost universal obsession with all things work–life balance. Especially if you are someone who either has or is expected to have caring responsibilities at some point.

Language matters most when it is so frequently used and widely understood. And work–life balance is *the* phrase, the touchstone, that conversations about the things so many of us care deeply about – happiness, fulfilment, impact, contribution, progress – centre around.

Psychologist Dr Alexandra Solomon writes about how *language shapes experience*, a message that is crucial for us to take to heart here. When we talk about balancing work and family, she says we 'plant a dangerous seed. We send a message that reinforces perfectionism and its trusty sidekick: inadequacy. Solomon reinforces that once we submit to the 'fantasy of balance' we begin to fall into a routine of working, paying bills and meeting the needs of our children, but that when this becomes unmanageable, we ultimately open ourselves up to shame and end up feeling like we are failing when we can't get the balance right.[7]

This point of language impacting experience is a powerful one. Researchers have further proved the link: a study into working mothers found that when 'employment' and 'mother-hood' were framed as complementary identities, the mothers' dual identity was explicitly beneficial to their well-being.[8] When the two were instead framed as conflicting roles, the mothers' work-related stress *increased*.

Language matters. Our mental models affect how we experience our real-world lives.

THE REPLACEMENT

So, in short, screw work–life balance. It is toxic. *Delete it.*

Instead, let's replace it with these four words: dashboard,

dials, levels and resilience. This is The Dials – a new mental model, a new approach to finding success in work and in life. *Your* Dials. Instead of the static, binary work–life balance bullshit, The Dials is a dynamic tool. It is both a snapshot of current times and a process to be worked through – step 1, step 2, step 3, and then a check for resilience. The Dials is a reflection of where you are at in this current moment, and a series of steps you can revisit in a discrete and/or continuous way from here on out:

(Dashboard | Dials | Levels) ^{Resilience}

- *Dashboard: who are you, what matters to you, what kind of life do you want to live, what do you want to achieve with it?* It starts with the dashboard itself. This contains your life goals, your values, your priorities: the things that make you uniquely you and speak to how you want to live your precious time on earth. This is an incredibly easy step to skip over, and the one which is missing from many conversations about life and work choices.
- *Dials: the component parts of living that life now and building it for the future.* Having a rich, varied and fulfilled life requires, yes *requires*, you to have multiple building blocks and expressions of what is on your dashboard. The lived, living, parts of a life and of how you are meeting your needs. You should have a dial for every component part of your life, at the appropriate detail and grouped together in meaningful ways that reflect how you are spending and want to spend your time.
- *Levels: consciously assessing what level each of your dials is set to and changing the intensity as needed.* This is a deliberate and intentional reflection of life *right now*. But the very nature of a dial – something designed to be adjusted – speaks to usability. You are going to be changing the settings on these dials

– dialling up or dialling down – as needs, opportunities, capacity and seasons of life change.

- **Resilience:** *are the choices you are making, both big and incremental, helping you optimise for resilience?* Resilience matters, in all its forms. When you consciously prioritise building it into your life it will manifest in the ability, the opportunity, to more frequently choose both which dials you have on your dashboard *and* the level at which those dials are set. That control itself has massive value. Uncertainty and change are intrinsic to the system we all operate in. We cannot plan for or choose everything that happens to us. This final piece of the framework is about working with this truth rather than fighting against it.

Over the next few chapters, we will cover each of these four sections of The Dials, one by one. Throughout each chapter are questions designed to help you think about what it all means for you in your unique life. As well as some more specific prompts to jot down notes for the basis of your Dials.

The Dials framework repeatedly and consistently helps me live my life in a way that is true to what is important to me. It keeps me honest about how I am using my time and helps me consciously choose what I am prioritising. It enables me to make sustainable choices in my life, and that supports my enjoyment of and fulfilment from it, and to roll with the punches when they inevitably come.

I hope it can do the same for you.

Chapter 2

YOUR DASHBOARD

I AM AN awful cook. There was a time when I tried to make myself some cheese on toast but didn't think about toasting the bread before putting the cheese on and putting it under the grill. Or the time I set burgers on fire by putting the oven on the wrong setting then leaving them in there for far too long. And the time I baked banana bread without any flour. And many more examples along these lines. I care about not being hungry, but not enough to do anything fancy about it.

It was an unexpected turn of events, therefore, when I found myself weighing up the respective benefits of accepting a position on the TV show *MasterChef* and accepting a job on the trading floor of a US bank to electronically buy and sell equities.

I, of course, wasn't the one being offered either opportunity, but I was in a conversation with Alexina, who was.

The question Alexina actually posed was whether I thought her career would take a hit if she was to ask for a four-day-a-week position at the investment bank so she could continue to pursue cooking. I asked a few more questions about the specifics, and then we launched into a fascinating back and forth about whether working flexibly in a corporate environment as a non-parent would be detrimental. About the relative merits of a day spent cooking or one tinkering with the speed at which an algorithm buys shares in Amazon. About career paths on the trading floor, about diversity and lifestyle and passions and money and all sorts.

Then I realised I hadn't asked, and Alexina hadn't offered, one vital piece of information: What was she trying to achieve here? Were we having a conversation about hobbies, or passions, or work, or income, or careers, or life goals or . . . or . . . or . . .?

It is obvious that days spent mixing ingredients or creating menus look very different to ones clicking between four giant computer screens while chatting furiously into a headset. And each of us will have a preference of course. But beyond the reality of those differences, and the importance of knowing ourselves well enough to understand which we will enjoy over the long term, are a set of needs that these career or life choices are intended to meet. Why was Alexina working at all? What did she need that career to produce to make it worth it for her, to make it sustainable enough so she could get to that outcome? What was she trying to do with her life? What were – are – her values? Her goals? Her priorities? Her needs?

We could – we did! – get totally lost in the specifics of this choice: the nuts and the bolts of hours worked versus the contents of the job versus different kinds of creativity versus money earned versus fun had, and on and on. When the truth is that there is no right answer. Only the right answer for each of us. Or, more accurately in this case, for Alexina.

When Alexina and I started getting into this, at a very surface level of course, everything changed. She began to articulate more about her background and her family circumstances. About her attitude to risk, about what recognition needed to look like to be meaningful to her, and about why she had found herself in the pretty unusual position of choosing between

29

baking and banking in the first place. And things started to become clearer. Not crystal clear mind you because #life. But clearer. And we'll get to what Alexina decided in the Conclusion (page 222).

For now, I tell this story as a microcosm of an essential missing piece of the conversation around all things career and work and fulfilment and life. It is so easy to skip ahead and weigh up the relative merits of specific options in front of us. Yet doing that only makes the decision harder, because we are weighing and measuring in a vacuum. The strengths and weaknesses of different options aren't objective facts: cooking isn't always more fun than banking, you don't always earn more money as a banker than a chef. There is no inherent worth or guaranteed higher standard of living if you do one or the other. Who is to say you are going to automatically maximise whatever metric you are solving for, in one place or another?

It is incredibly hard to give good advice to others and often ourselves about what to do (or not do!) without thinking deeply about what is important to us and what we are trying to achieve, in the very broadest sense of the word. For some, it might be something as abstract as curiosity. Others meanwhile might be driven by the very concrete, like wanting to work for themselves or affording to live in a particular area near family. Some thrive in a large, complex organisation full of large complex people and problems. Others need to be outside every day, or only answer to themselves. Some need to create. Others need to fix. Many are happy to go with the flow, while others strive to do nothing of the sort.

We each need to spend time thinking about who we, uniquely, are. About what we value and what our values are. About what our goals are, short and long term. About what resources and opportunities and advantages we already have to hand, and what obstacles and barriers might be in our way. About what, out of all these things, is changeable and what is not, by us or others. About what we are trying to achieve. About what matters to us and what kind of life we want to live. About what success looks like for us and us alone, both in the here and now and in the future. About what we want life to look like, to feel like, to truly be.

This is your dashboard. This is your foundation.

Each of these points is difficult to even start thinking about, even more so as a whole. Helpfully, there is plenty of research and expertise we can draw on to help us do this.

LIFE GOALS AND PRIORITIES

Welcome to my happy place: planning.

When an interviewer asks me where I see myself in five years, I eat that question for breakfast. Five years? Pah. I went through a stage of having the next 15 planned out in a spreadsheet. Thankfully, I grew out of that fairly destructive habit. But still, I have anywhere from three to 10 unofficial versions running in my head at any given moment. From the ludicrous but fun (what I'd do if I won the lottery ... especially ludicrous given I don't buy lottery tickets), to the vaguely possible but mostly improbable, to the scary and macabre (what I would do if <insert-person-I-love-so-much-I-can't-even-write-their-name-here> died). It's that last one that really tells you the most about me when it comes to all things planning. Even when it's for the absolute worst, the thing you cannot even put into words, nine times out of 10 I've thought about it and have a workable plan about how I'd approach the obvious bits of what would happen next. There was even a time in my early twenties when I had a plan of where my then-boyfriend and I would escape to out of London if there was some kind of city-based apocalypse and we needed to hide out in the countryside for some years. Yep, I am one of life's planners.

So, *of course*, I would recommend spending some time thinking about both what your goals are for the future and what you can/will do to make them happen. Ambitions, dreams, hopes for the future, life plans, five-year plans, all of that good stuff goes right here. And not just because I enjoy it, but because it verifiably works.

In the sixties, American psychologist Edwin Locke began researching and writing his now-renowned academic works on the goal-setting theory of motivation, and over the following 60 years he collected inordinate amounts of data about how the theory really works. His thesis centres on the fact that goal setting is both a foundational and essential component of so-called 'task performance', which I am going to simply translate as 'doing stuff well'. Locke's proven insight is that setting specific and challenging goals, and ones where you can get appropriate feedback on your route to completing them, contributes to better outcomes. The insight of Locke's which really gets me is this: that 'people must choose to discover what is beneficial to their welfare, they must set goals to achieve it, they must choose the means for attaining these goals, and then they must choose to act on the basis of these judgements'.[1] **Goals motivate action.** Feedback on that action helps you find the ones that really make a difference in reaching that goal. And there we have the virtuous circle of progress.

Note that this is the precise opposite approach to 'manifesting'. Whether you achieve your dreams or not isn't about whether you mood-boarded them hard enough. Wishing for things does not make them come true, despite what far too many charlatans on the internet will tell you, or rather sell you a course on. But knowing what you want to happen, taking steps to make it happen and checking in with both yourself and outside feedback sources along the way really does.

Identifying your goals

Planning for the future isn't about locking yourself into a particular path, spending hours and hours studiously going through worksheets which you never glance at again or trying to predict the unpredictable (the one thing life is guaranteed to be).

The ability to flex and reframe plans is what is powerful. This is not about getting 'it' perfect or executing 'it' perfectly. This is about creating space to find and solidify the convictions of your most rational, best self, in your calmest, clearest moments – a touchstone to return to when the fog of daily life descends.

Maybe it's a really clear #lifegoal or a sensible/ambitious career plan. Maybe it's the articulation of a feeling or a set of feelings you want to cultivate throughout your life. A friend, Tom, in a conversation about all things Dials said that he would have one word on his dashboard: adventure. Maybe it's concrete things like kids or marriage, or their less tangible cousin, love. Maybe it's a state, like friendship or grounded-ness. Or some of the things that may help you get there: money, freedom . . . Or perhaps the things that you would 'spend' that on: living somewhere sunny or snowy, or the chance to be creative, or outside, or snuggled up with a book every day. Maybe it's a contribution like kindness or furthering a cause that is important to you.

What immediately comes to mind for you? Something I've listed already? Or are you aggrieved I've left something fundamental to you out of these examples?

33

Don't worry about getting too specific. We, collectively, are stunningly bad at predicting future preferences. There is extensive behavioural literature on people's self-predictions of their future preferences and how we almost always get it wrong.[2] We're worse at thinking about how our own preferences will change, than those of others, and we are rubbish at predicting futures that don't benefit us.[3,4] Not only that, but there are literally thousands of academic articles looking at the difference between stated and revealed preferences, i.e., the differences between what we say we want and then what we go on to choose or do.

This isn't about pinning down the exact job, or the exact hobby, or the exact pet or house or type of business you want. If you try to optimise for a very specific outcome then it doesn't take much to knock you off course. If you instead optimise for a wide set of outcomes along some key themes – like community, or family, or freedom, or safety – then you are building in resilience for everything the world can throw at you. There are likely to be a million (billion?) different paths your life can take. And you want to be fulfilled in as many of them as possible. We will also come back to this resilience point in a lot more depth when we discuss the fourth step of The Dials (see Chapter 5).

I would, however, really encourage you to be bold here. Think about what you truly want, not what you have been told to want or not want. Which isn't easy, I know, thanks to human genetic code developed over hundreds of thousands of years to support the objective of survival. To serve that end, we learned it's safer to be a member of a tribe. It is easier to imagine ourselves wanting and doing all the things that we see thousands and millions of humans before us have done and are currently around us doing. This is a mostly unconscious instinct and one which kicks in most when we feel at risk, which you will as soon as you step out of that tribe-defined safety zone.

World-renowned investor Warren Buffett has spoken of a technique that helps him on this front. A principle that enables him to believe in himself and in investment decisions when others had given up: the 'inner scorecard'. When you have an inner scorecard, you and you alone define success for yourself.

Buffet describes the conundrum we all face as such: 'Would you rather be the world's greatest lover, but have everyone think you're the world's worst lover? Or would you rather be the world's worst lover but have everyone think you're the world's greatest lover? Now, that's an interesting question. Here's another one. If the world couldn't see your results, would you rather be thought of as the world's greatest investor but in reality, have the world's worst record? Or be thought of as the world's worst investor when you were the best?'[5] Your dashboard is not about how the world sees you or thinks of you, or how you, or what you have, or what you have done or will do stacks up against others. It is about your metrics alone, even if one of those metrics is an element of recognition from others.

Being mortgage-free by 30 was one of the goals I articulated to myself when I first got that City job at the end of my university degree. Spoiler: I am firmly over 30 and firmly still in possession of a rather large mortgage. But the values behind that goal are still very much in play. The goal itself was too specific, too prescriptive, and incredibly naïve. But now I realise that what I was trying to articulate was a priority of family and the time, space and security to enjoy them. That was – is – absolutely a guiding light for me. I want to raise my nice kids alongside my nice husband in a nice part of the world unthreatened (yet) by extreme weather or politics, or risks to the rule of law. It sounds yawn-inducingly vanilla, I know. I don't think we've reached the stage where wanting a nice place to raise a nice family is subversive enough to warrant it being called 'bold', as I urged you to be a few paragraphs ago, but if I was being guided by an outer scorecard it would be easy enough to be embarrassed by that vanilla classification. Luckily, I have had some time to really work to accept the inner scorecard concept and test the hypothesis of whether the nice house and nice kids and nice husband bring fulfilment for me. And, dear reader, they do.

It's not easy to say out loud that you might not want kids when that is what most people go on to do. It's not easy to admit that you want to be CEO of a Fortune 500 company when you know how few people will make that aim come to pass. It is not easy to eschew the expensive schools or holidays or cars your neighbours are all purchasing when you know those things, or the things you would have to do to attain them, would not fill you up. It is not easy to tell people – or indeed yourself – you'd rather have a job than a career, or a career over a family, or family over either, or none of those things at all. Because almost all of us feel the pressure to conform. And this is absolutely where we shouldn't.

The purpose here is to have a sense of clarity about who you are and what you want. Knowing this is going to help you when the going gets tough, when you are wavering or questioning. And for when the going is good too – those times when you have the first-class, but still true, problem of too many wonderful options.

Questions to ask yourself
- If a genie popped up next to you and granted you three wishes, Disney style, what would you ask for?
- What do your answers say about what is important to you?

_____

_____

_____

_____

Joel

It depends on how extensive my asks could be! I'm going to go big . . .

I'd like to grow old, happily, in my marriage and see my kids grow up. I want them to have their own successful families and lives. It's the one thing I'd really like. I know it's more likely than not, but I worry about, or rather think about, a catastrophe. So, if I had a wish, it would be that.

My second would be to feel I had applied my skills at a sufficiently senior level in my career and done some good by doing so.

My third . . . a personal one would be about staying fit and healthy. A bigger picture one would be to do with the state of UK politics and the world. Things feel grim right now. Am I allowed four wishes?! And maybe these aren't all that big after all.

These wishes do speak to what is important to me. Thinking about it now, it's surprising to me that there isn't something in there about friends, given how essential they are to me. But maybe I don't need to wish for that because I already have them. Still, they are important, very much so.

37

Using your dashboard as a commitment device
Your dashboard can be a wonderful commitment device. It can keep you aligned with the things that you truly want and care about, as well as making the outcomes you are aiming for more likely. The knowledge in and of itself of what you care about is massively valuable. It is the benchmark against which you can compare your actions, your direction and your location, as choices, opportunities and calamities come your way.

One of my favourite examples of this comes courtesy of the economist Steven Levitt, the co-author of the *Freakonomics* books, and an award-winning academic specialising in the field of crime. Steven tells a story of how, as he began to find his feet in the early days of his economics career, he realised that he wanted to do whatever research interested him, and not worry about the implications for his career or the like. He did this by designing and implementing a so-called 'commitment device': where you are taking an action now that rules out future options that might seem attractive. He deliberately decided not to pay his children's nannies' social security; something he knew would rule him out of ever getting a senate confirmable position in the US government (a career goal of many a professional economist). He knew enough about himself that he might be swayed at some point by such an offer, but that he would be both bad at the job itself and the potential of this outcome would steer him from a path which would bring him the most fulfilment – writing his bold research. This ultimately led him to his current occupation as an author and podcaster. 'I *wanted* a tarnished record, just in case one day I was overcome by temporary insanity and deluded myself into thinking I should take a high-ranking government job,' he says.[7]

While I love Steve Levitt's example, I wouldn't necessarily recommend something that drastic for everyone. Because the reality is that these plans, these goals, your dashboard can, will and *should* change. The 23-year-old version of you is a different one to the 53-year-old. The one who has lost a job knows much more about how stressful, or not, that experience is for you and your specific life circumstances. The version who lived on that beach and missed the city is different to the one who went back and realised that the place wasn't the problem, but the people were.

The goal of all this planning and shaping isn't to wrench you consistently away from the present or to pretend that you can truly control what comes next in your life. It is to empower you with the knowledge that you've done what you can. It is to give justice to the idea that there is both something you can do about the future but that obsessing about it can be the very thing which stops the best bits happening. True enlightenment is supposedly reached when one is able to let go of both the past and future and live only in the present. These are challenges that Zen Buddhist monks have dedicated their entire lives to conquering, as have the Taoists and the Stoicists and philosophers such as Aristotle and Hadot. The rest of us might need to give those other time states a little bit of attention to enable us to give the present the time and the acknowledgement it deserves.

MORE THAN JUST GOALS: VALUES AND RESOURCES

There is a reason I am not calling this section 'goal setting' or making it solely about objectives or aims, or even hopes and dreams. **Your dashboard needs to be more than just what you *want*. It needs to include some honest reflection about the kind of person you are, your genuine needs and real commitments, and the values you hold most dear**, as well as the resources you have at your disposal to make your wants happen, and the means you can, and will, deploy to get there.

When I was at school, a new girl joined our year group after her family moved from America. Annis was in possession of the biggest personality this group of painfully self-aware English teenagers had ever seen. She was so confident, so funny, so relaxed and was, of course, up to date on all the latest trends out of the USA. In the era of dial-up internet and *Friends* being broadcast weekly, this only added to the aura of cool around her. In short, we lapped her up.

When Annis told us she was going to be a singer, there wasn't a single moment of doubt among us all that this was going to happen. Until she let go her first rendition of Britney/ N*Sync/Destiny's Child or whatever teeny-bopper pop we were obsessed with at the time. As Annis could not sing a note. Literally.

This wasn't just, 'eek, there are better singers out there' territory or something some lessons could fix. She was truly tone deaf. She laughed it all off and in true American-dream style told us it was still going to happen.

Scroll forwards a decade or two and Annis has gone on to be a very successful graphic designer.

This story sits neatly in the par-for-the-course-teenage-self-discovery bucket, and I am sure we each have a similar tale or two of the disconnect between what we thought we could do as youngsters and what we could actually do. A few months or years spent dreaming of being a popstar as a teenager are unlikely to do anyone any harm after all.

Yet, this is the pickle that many of us find ourselves in time and time again. We are often asked what we want to be when we grow up – an important question no doubt. But how often are we asked about the kind of person we are, the talents or skills we are in possession of to start with, about who we want to be or what talents and skills we want to hone or develop along the way? How often are we asked about whether we have the means to do so now or the wherewithal to get the means to do so in the future? How often are we supported to develop the self-aware-ness or self-knowledge to ask these questions of ourselves, forget about taking the actions that those answers then prompt?

Your dashboard should speak to the ends you are aiming for, absolutely. But also, who you are, who you want to be and what means you can – and will – deploy to make all of this happen.

Another achingly vanilla truth about who I am and how I like to live is that, whisper it quietly, I really, really like work-ing in an office. Hell, I even quite like meetings! I like being warm and dry and wearing nice clothes, even if the high heels got ditched when I returned after my first maternity leave. I like getting paid to solve complicated problems, alongside really smart people, all under some pressure but knowing that life and death it is not. I like being myself all day, coming home to my own house and seeing the people I care about at the end of it. Things I couldn't do all day every day would be travelling or performing or having singular moments that would make, or break, my career. As a suspense-intolerant person, simply watching athletes line up at the Olympics makes my stomach churn.

Working out these kinds of honest truths about yourself and how you like to spend the day-to-day of life are essential to getting your dashboard right. Just because you can, doesn't always mean you should.

Questions to ask yourself

- Can you think of a time when those around you were telling you something was a perfect fit – a school subject, or a job, or a hobby perhaps – and you just knew it wasn't right, despite their insistence, and your no doubt strong performance?
- Does an aspect of someone else's life that everyone seems to covet give you the heebie-jeebies?
- What are those things that feel weird to say out loud about what you will, and will not, can, or cannot do to live a happy life?

_____

_____

_____

_____

Kate

The thing that leaps out for me here is kids. I know a lot of people are going to have that as a goal for their lives, but I envision myself as being child-free by choice. Well, I already am, but I mean staying that way. It just doesn't feel right for me. I want to keep my time as my own and think – know – I can do the caring I want to do in other ways. Whereas I don't think I could do the other things I want in life – travel, sleep, work – in other ways if I was a parent.

Taylor Swift is clearly a phenomenal singer, songwriter and guitarist. She has clocked up nine number ones on the US Billboard 200, putting her just behind the likes of Elvis Presley and Eminem (ten-a-piece).[8] Her mother recounts how at 12 years old Taylor became fixated with a 12-string guitar and how they had told her she would not be able to play it until she was much older. But this only spurred Taylor on to learn to play it: 'Don't ever say never or can't do to Taylor. She started playing it four hours a day – six on the weekends. She would get calluses on her fingers, and they would crack and bleed, and we would tape them up and she'd just keep on playing.' She was clearly someone who had very clear goals about what she wanted to do with all this talent, and was prepared to do the needed hard work at a very early age. Taylor herself tells a story of visiting Nashville record companies aged 11: 'my mom waited in the car with my little brother while I knocked on doors up and down Music Row. I would say, "Hi, I'm Taylor. I'm 11; I want a record deal. Call me".'[9]

Taylor knew what talents she had, and who/what she wanted to be. And she was extraordinarily bold about marshalling, let's be totally honest here, massively unusual levels of resources available to her to make that happen (her father worked in high finance). She persuaded her parents to relocate to the periphery of Nashville, the home of country music, when she was 13 years old: 'I decided to move to Nashville when I was about 10 years old. I was obsessed with watching biography TV shows about Faith Hill and Shania Twain, and I noticed that both went to Nashville to start their careers.'[10] Taylor then relentlessly pestered her parents and they began to visit Nashville more and more often. When she got a deal with a major record label three years later, her parents gave in and the family relocated there.

I certainly wouldn't have had the gumption to persuade my parents to move across the country when I was a very young teenager. And neither would my parents have had the resources or careers which could facilitate doing so.

It is not always enough to be good at the *thing*: the singing, the selling, the caring, the creating, the lawyering, the

43

patience to be with small children for 12 hours a day, whatever it is. You must have both the ability and the resources to use it. You also need to be able to apply your talent in a specific way. You might be a wonderful singer but have zero cares to travel around the world performing. You might design amazing clothes but lack the ability to put together a show and build that into a brand, but thrive at an established label. The necessary skills and temperament to do work in a particular way are themselves a key component.

Taking stock
We each came, or are coming, into adulthood with a variety of different privileges and barriers: gender, race, nationality, wealth, family stability, education, network, natural talent, personality, lived experiences, the social and political policies of where we live ... The list can go on. As we grow, we collect, define and maybe escape pieces of these along the way. Some for the better, some for the worse.

I don't raise this to suggest that part of each of us – our identities, realities, circumstances or dreams – are either trivial, or insurmountable, or indeed manifest destiny. However, as an example, it is both easier and more rational to take big risks if you have a big safety net in place. You can do more in a company or a city in which it is safe to be your authentic self, but that is more or less likely in different places and with different identities. These things have a bearing on each of us.

I wouldn't be writing this book if it wasn't for the change in parental leave policies in the UK in 2015. The fact that my husband has been able to take six months off alongside me each time we have had a child has given me, us, our children, the immeasurable joy of time together. And lots of measurable things as well: one of which was the freedom to write my first book about yoga self-practice, which in turn led me to be able to get the deal and begin to write this one on my second leave. What was once a barrier (unequal parental leave laws) changed over time, and then became a privilege (versus those raising families in the USA for example).

It is surprisingly rare that we are encouraged to do a stock-check of the privileges and barriers, both personal and societal. It is even rarer that we are asked to think about how each or all of them interact with the nature of the society and time that we exist in and then, in turn, with our hopes or plans for our lives.

This is what the second half of this book is for. Together we will examine the many areas of life this covers. I want you to have these questions in your mind before we launch in and try to work out *your* answers, together.

CREATING YOUR DASHBOARD

Now over to you – let's start sketching out your dashboard. Start by thinking about, or writing down some thoughts about, your values, your current and future priorities for your life, and your goals.

It can be as detailed, or not, as you like.

Author Ryan Holiday describes his three priorities in life in four unique words: great writer, great marriage, great father.[11]

Here are some prompts to get you started:

Dashboard prompts

Who are you?

- What kind of person are you?
- What matters to you?
- What interests you?
- What are your values?

What ends are you aiming for?

- What are you trying to achieve?
- What are your goals – short- and long-term – for your life?
- What kind of life do you want to live?
- What does success look for you? Today, in 5 years, in 10 and in 30?

What means can you, will you, deploy to reach those ends?

- What resources, opportunities and advantages do you have?
- What obstacles and barriers may be in your way?
- How changeable are all of these? By you, by others?
- Do you have or can you create the skills, temperament and opportunities to do what is required?

Lastly, one final zoom out for perspective:

- What do you want life to . . .
  - o . . . look like?
  - o . . . feel like?
  - o . . . be?

Nic

What matters to me is time with my family, security in my life and building something of value in my work – something that has intrinsic value. This has become my business, though that was not obvious to me when I was starting out in the world of work some 15 years ago. I wanted – want – to build something that was flexible with my life but that has value. I don't want work to mean I have sacrificed my personal life. Not least of all because I want to be both supported by and be supportive of my friends and family.

Your dashboard recap

Your dashboard is the foundation of the mental model for your life. Your touchstone that reflects who you are, your goals, your priorities, your values and the resources available to you to make it all happen. It can be an evolving commitment device and an inspiration.

Chapter 3

YOUR DIALS

———————

PHASE TWO OF The Dials uppercase, is the dials, lowercase.

This is where we move from those big-picture brushstrokes that we explored in the previous chapter to the actual components that make up a life; out of the theoretical into the practical. All the airy-fairy stuff is great (seriously, did I tell you about how much I love 10-year 'plans', no matter how likely they are to come true or be needed?), it is totally and utterly essential no less, but we all live in the here and now. We are each allocating our precious time and energy on specific areas of our lives in this very moment. By creating dials to sit on our dashboard, we can consciously express how those priorities, goals and values that we sketched out translate into how we spend our time. We also officially get to throw out that ludicrous binary of work versus life. And, with it, any hint that 'balance' is either possible or preferable.

Here, we are expressing your life as its component parts. Each will be its own dial. In total, we are aiming for a handful or two. Together these dials represent both what is important to us and what we are doing about it, day-to-day, week-to-week, month-to-month and year-to-year.

WHAT ARE YOUR DIALS?

There is a stunning amount of consistency when it comes to what humans want and also need to have in their lives.

The Pew Research Center, a world-leading data-driven social science research organisation, released a study in late 2021 into what makes life meaningful.[1] They asked nearly 19,000 adults across 17 advanced economies open-ending questions, and entire cohort's responses were grouped using the median percentages across the 17 groups of respondents into the following 16 categories, the first few of which – family and children, occupation and career accounted for 63 per cent of respondents.

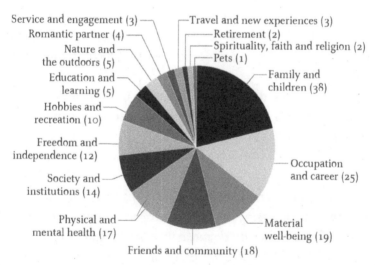

Source: Chart, author's own based on data from the Pew Research Centre

Looking at the data, it is fascinating to see both further similarities and deeper disparities. Occupation was one of the top three sources of meaning for people in most places included in the survey. Yet, 43 per cent of Italians ranked it as top three versus just six per cent of people in South Korea, where the linked-but-distinct priority of material well-being came out most highly ranked. Similarly, in health, only six per cent specified it as a source of meaning in Taiwan, yet 48 per cent did in Spain – making it the top source of meaning there. Topics like friends, education and hobbies were much more often sources of meaning for the under-thirties than the over-sixties, for whom health and retirement featured much more regularly. The United Kingdom, Australia, France, New Zealand and Sweden all placed a relatively high emphasis on nature over other countries; making one of the top eight sources of meaning, independently from the category of hobbies and recreation that it would be easy to assume it fell into. As much as I love my cats, I can't say they would warrant a standalone 'Pets' entry in the list of what makes my life meaningful, though they did for nearly 2,000 respondents. Which is the entire point . . .

Our individual dials will be unique to us, even if the broadest version of a list from which they are drawn will look similar.

James

I'm quite introverted at heart. Most of the time, I'm not too worried about seeing my friends every week. What I do try to, well, not try, what I do make time for is a couple of weekends a year where this group of us from school go away together. We are spread all over now and living really different lives. We don't do anything fancy, but it's seen us through all sorts.

Below are some prompts to get you started: are any of these *your* dials? You'll see higher level categories on the left, which can be a dial or dials themselves, and more detailed categories on the right. These are, however, simple initial suggestions. The dials *and* their groupings *and* their level of detail are changeable.

Work	Job
	Career
	Education & Learning
Relationships	Partner
	Children
	Family
	Friends
	Pets
Self	Physical Health
	Fitness
	Mental Health
	Spirituality, Faith, Religion
Leisure	Hobby
	Travel
	Culture
	Creativity
	Nature
Society	Community
	Impact
Other	One-off Projects
	Money

Each can be approached in a multitude of ways. Take 'Friends' for example. This could be a single dial or it could be three: one each for school, university and work friends.

Similarly, maybe having fitness and physical health split out makes no sense to you because your Pilates classes and running sessions are the way you look after your physical health. Or maybe it really chimes true: as someone who has experienced a health crisis or two, and birthing a child or two, it does for me. When I was recovering from having each of my sons, the very best thing I could do for my physical health was absolutely zero fitness for a period of weeks or months. And then, as I healed, they merged back into one dial. And if we looked back to my early twenties, I had neither a fitness nor physical health dial at all. The nonchalance of youth!

The detail of each category can, should and will vary for each of us full stop, and for each of us at different times, to help us get the dials which are right just for us.

Thinking about our dials congregating in little groups on our dashboard can help too. Because who is to say that Education & Learning is always for your work? A part-time MBA could be to help secure the next big work promotion. Or maybe it's a passion project. Learning Italian in your free time simply because you love it, is a hobby. Or maybe it is because there is a piece of your dashboard which is all about retiring to a little hilltop Italian town, so it's about Leisure. Or is it because your partner is Italian and you want to speak to their, soon to be your, family, so it's relationship related? These are incredibly personal and totally specific to you.

These are not questions to which the answers are set in stone. The set-up of your dials is not permanent. Quite the opposite – you can take dials on and off your dashboard as life changes.

Sometimes a dial or two will be removed or added forever (kids being an example of a permanent one, even if the reality of parenting small children is going to look very different to being a parent to adults). At other times you are going to create space for a new dial for a period knowing that it will get removed again at a point in the future: perhaps it is a house renovation, or planning a wedding, or taking on extra shifts to reach a financial milestone.

Knowing this can be an incredibly helpful sense-check for evaluating new projects or opportunities or demands on your time.

Questions to ask yourself
- Do you have space to add a new dial to your life right now?
- Do you even want to?
- Do you need to remove another dial to make that possible?
- What are the most important parts of your life right now?

Wei

I've recently added a new dial to my group of work-related dials. I am a barrister and I am consciously working towards becoming Kings Counsel, or 'taking silk' as they say. This is basically becoming the most senior type of barrister. To do that, I am taking cases as part of the government panel. This means doing more work for lower rates (the government rate is about 10 per cent of my commercial one) in order to get more experience and build my profile. Becoming KC would be a huge achievement – the pinnacle of most barristers' legal careers. And it would mean all my rates would ultimately be higher, but that is

> *not why I am doing it per se: the status appeals of course, but the intellectual rigour and achievement is a huge part, as are the cases it would make available to me in the future. It's several years' work to even be considered, but thinking about it separately to my current case work is a really helpful, and frankly important, distinction.*

To get this book into your hands, I had a 'write the goddamn book' dial on my dashboard for a couple of years (well, that was what it was called on a bad day. It was just a 'write the book' dial most of the time). If you are reading this, it means I finished it and that dial is now off my dashboard. Though more accurately has reincarnated in its new form: 'help get the book out there', the form of which I'm not quite sure about at this stage.

WORKING YOUR DIALS

There are three reasons why getting your dials, your groupings and the right level of detail *for you, at the moment* helps.

Firstly, having the right dials in place is the mental prompt to adjust the levels on each of them, deliberately and consciously. This action – this intentional mental action of dialling one component part of your life up or another down – is so much more productive and calming than trying to aim for the ever-impossible static status of 'balance'.

As I said, this book was its own dial for over two years. Those years contained a chunk of the COVID-19 pandemic, being pregnant for the third time and giving birth to my second baby, shielding at home for months while my husband and I both worked and looked after our toddler alone, a second shared parental leave and a second return to work. The only way this book happened is because I had the dial on my dashboard.

That, though, is an essential but insufficient step. Because there were many days and months in those years when I did precisely *zero* work on this book. The book dial was turned all the way down. There were others when it hummed away on a low-to-medium setting: maybe I did a call with my agent or read a book for research purposes. And others when it was turned up full blast: days ferreted away from kids and laundry and anything except writing and writing. The next chapter – Your Levels – is all about this dialling up and dialling down. **For now, know that the better reflection your dials are of what is in your life and how you think about those pieces, the more impactful the dialling up and down will be.**

Secondly, getting your dials, your groupings and your level of detail right *for you, at the moment* is important as it works backwards: linking your dials back to your dashboard. Being honest with yourself about what you are doing with your time, and how you are allocating your other resources, is at the core of The Dials as a mental model, as a way of approaching life. The little group of dials you have which represent work, or self, or relationships are a quick spot-check on whether what you are doing every day speaks to what life you think you want to build. If that retire-to-an-Italian-hilltop dream is real and meaningful for you and takes up a big piece of your dashboard, is it worrying for you that there isn't a single dial on that dashboard which is helping you get closer to it? Or maybe it's not that much of a priority after all, at least right now? There is no judgement here and there are no right answers, but this can be valuable feedback if you do the reconciliation every now and again.

Your dials will help you live in the present
The philosopher Søren Kierkegaard, he of existential crisis fame, expresses this backwards–forwards dichotomy neatly: 'it is quite true what Philosophy says: that Life must be understood

backwards. But that makes one forget the other saying: that it must be lived – forwards'.[2] Yet, there is something missing in the middle. Something that the hyphen is not doing justice to. Something that needs explicitly spelling out: the present.

The right now.

Yep, this minute.

As.

You.

Read.

These.

Words.

Yes, get your groupings right and sense-check that the dials represent your dashboard priorities. Yes, spend time thinking about what the right level of detail is so that you have the right dials to adjust up and down when needed. Yet the *most* important part of the dials – this second step of The Dials – is all about the present. Having the right dials on your dashboard can help you do the actual living.

The Kierkegaard quote I shared above continues with this: 'The more one ponders this, the more it comes to mean that life in the temporal existence never becomes quite intelligible, precisely because at no moment can I find complete quiet to take the backward-looking position.' I won't lie and say I could disentangle the meaning of this at first, or even second or third read. My interpretation now though is that life happens, by definition, in a series of connected 'right now' moments, making it very hard to find enough time to look back and understand ourselves or our purpose. The dashboard is incomplete, but hopefully practical, attempt to address the challenges posed by understanding ourselves or our purpose. But what floors me is that Kierkegaard could 'at no moment . . . find complete quiet' for sufficient self-reflection. Kierkegaard did not have time to find quiet?! If this is hard for a world-famous philosopher, I think we can all be a bit gentler on ourselves when we struggle too.

We get it, don't we? We get that we are meant to be living in the present and meditating and yoga-ing and what-have-you. But, then, why is it so hard to do?

Meditation – the very practice of living in the present – is scientifically proven to 'work'. Randomised control trials show that it has a beneficial effect on anxiety symptoms and improves stress reactivity and coping.[3] There is further evidence that it has beneficial effects on attention, memory, verbal fluency, executive function, processing speed, overall cognitive flexibility and even creativity.[4] Yet, over 90 per cent of users who started using the two premier meditation apps, Headspace and Calm, stopped just a month later.[5] That is a lot of broken new year's resolutions.

Despite having fallen in love with yoga, spent years extolling its virtues to hundreds of thousands of people on social media and written a book on both the magic and the practicalities of independent yoga practice, I still find it hard to step on my mat as much as I would like to. I skip my practice entirely many, many days, sometimes weeks, telling myself I need to work or spend more time with my kids (even though I do both of those things better once I've practised). I hop on my Peloton bike or go for a walk to tick the physical movement box, knowing that it is not the same thing. Knowing that the only person – mind, soul – I am short-changing is myself.

The reason I don't practise as much yoga as I would like to, the reason this becomes more and more true the more I need the calm and presence that yoga brings to me is this: it is *so frickin' hard* to be on my mat with my thoughts, to just be in the present – with the criticisms of not having got there sooner; with the snarky comments to myself about why I am wobbling or why I can't do the pose I could do last week; with the nagging feeling

I should be tackling several entries on my to-do list. Until I stay. And breathe. And do the pose as my body needs it today. Reminding myself in the process that those comments are not universal truths, that I can let them come and go and be OK – be better, rather, because I did. That my to-do list isn't me, that my worth is not defined by my productivity. And for a moment in time – the moment even Kirkegaard struggled to find – I find peace.

And then days, and sometimes weeks, go by and I don't get my mat out.

And it all starts again.

Ultimately, if the living in the now was easy, we would all already be doing it – by default. It is hard because it is valuable, and it is valuable because it is hard. **My hope with the dials is that they can be one more, small, but useable, weapon in your arsenal for living in the present.** That, by looking at how you are spending the actual moments of your actual life, you can sense-check that you are living as you wish. Right here, right now. That the things you spend your day, your week, your month on are the things that make life worth living.

Pause here. Look back at the previous week. If that week was going to get repeated again and again over the next five years, would it be a fair reflection of what your dashboard is all about, what you want your life to be all about? Yes? No? What about the past month, or six months, or year? I ask these questions not because every day, or week, or month, or even year has to be this perfect representation of everything we have ever wanted or indeed will want, but because all we have are these days, weeks, months, years. As they happen.

Therefore, I have a yoga dial, and a kids dial, and a husband dial among all the ones about career and book-writing and so on. They were all once ambitions, dreams, for my life. And now they are here, some hard-fought for, some which I lucked into pretty wild ways. And I use my dials to remind me of that. I need to enjoy them right here, right now. Not just for the piece of my dashboard that they are fulfilling or whatever plans and dreams I have for us all in the future.

Joan Didion says it better than I ever could. The American writer shared these thoughts on living life at a graduation ceremony in 1975: 'I'm not telling you to make the world better, because I don't think that progress is necessarily part of the package. I'm just telling you to live in it.'[6] Her profound philosophy is based upon the fact that we can only do the things that make a life worth living when we are doing precisely that – alive. So we should sing and write and embrace our children now, while we have that wonderful chance.

CREATING YOUR DIALS
Step 1: Start your list
Jot down a list of the component parts of your life you already have, the ones you may want to be spending time on and the ones you need – in any order, zero judgement at all.

Dial prompts
- What things have you spent time on in the past day?
- What things have you spent time on in the past week?
- What things have you spent time on in the past month?
- What things have you spent time on in the past year?
- What do you wish you had spent time on but haven't?
- What is coming up in the future that will require your time?

These can be concrete activities, or people, or values, or projects. Anything goes. Refer to the list on page 51 for help.

Step 2: Create groupings

Take that initial list and rewrite it, this time grouping relevant dials together. The categories I suggested on page 51 (work, relationships, leisure, self, society, other) may be helpful, or they may not be. But the dials in each group should relate both to each other and to something that you spelled out in your dashboard. For example, if a dashboard value for you is 'adventure', what are the dials that speak to that? If a goal on your dashboard is 'financial security', then you might have a few dials in this group: your current job, your side hustle, your savings dial and your investment dial. If 'family' features big on your dashboard, how is that showing up for you in your dials?

Step 3: Add detail

Do you need any extra detail here? If you have one 'work' dial, I would really encourage you to be more specific: work is never one thing. Yes, it is the job you may have right now, but it could be the next promotion or project, or the side hustle that will one day become a business, or the training you are taking, or the books you are reading to help you do your best in your role.

Similarly, zooming out a little in some areas can help. Let's take Leisure. You don't have to have four specified and perfect hobbies lined up. Having fun at the weekend is a great priority, full stop.

Your dials recap

Your dials are about expressing your life as an expansive list of its component parts: how you are spending your time now and how you want to be – each as its own dial. Together, these handful or two of dials represent both what is important to you and what you are doing about it, day-to-day, week-to-week, month-to-month and year-to-year.

Work, relationships, self-expression and self-care, how you spend your leisure time, what brings you joy and where you develop your passions, how you create impact in the world, how you participate in your community, as well as all the special projects or current priorities that life throws up – moving house, planning a wedding, sorting out your retirement savings, helping a friend survive through the immediate aftermath of a divorce – these can all be dials on your dashboard.

Thinking about the right groupings for your dials, and the right level of detail for your dials, can further help too. Friends or money will be one dial for some, or more for others. Framing that side hustle as part of your work group can remind you it is a valid and important way to spend your time, and help you create the boundary you need to say no in your main job.

Chapter 4

YOUR LEVELS

'BULLSHIT.'

This was the general, and often more specific, response I would get when I answered 'I don't' to the thorniest of thorny questions that women seem to get asked more than anyone else. The 'How do you do it all?' one. Because I was getting a lot done and, seemingly, not blowing myself up. Which itself is indicative of two truths. Firstly, that no one is as aware of your mistakes as you are. Because I was *definitely* blowing myself up as I worked out the second truth: that there was another way.

The 'a lot' I was getting done at the time looked impressive from the outside. And, honestly, felt pretty good from the inside too. I was approaching 10 years of my career in investment banking and, having moved roles internally a couple of years previously, had hit my stride doing a job that truly suited my skills. After the inevitable slog of the first few years of any big career, and seven years of being in a seat where I was good enough but not outright *good*, suddenly I got what it was to *enjoy* working.

Over the same time frame, I took up yoga and it fast became 'a thing', on several fronts. My start with the practice was stunningly inauspicious: no history of dance or gymnastics, or even basic sport as a child. Instead, after cycling five miles to and from work for all of six months, I was hit by a white van and scraped off the central London tarmac by two lovely paramedics. I was lucky in the grand scheme of things: a broken right collarbone, a few hand spans of missing skin and some soft tissue damage to my right shoulder. After a few months of going to a weekly phys-iotherapy treatments and studiously doing absolutely none of the homework exercises I was set, my physio told me we'd run out of sessions. She thought I should try something like yoga as it would help my mobility while hopefully capturing my attention enough to get some consistency going. Little did she know how right she would be!

Within a year I was taking classes and/or practising multi-ple times a week, and over the next 18 months of sharing my progressively less awkward and stiff home yoga practice on Instagram, I'd gained over 100,000 followers, done my yoga teaching training and started teaching both a regular class at a local studio and my own workshops on yoga self-practice.

It looked like, and some days felt like, I was getting 'it all' done. Living the dream, right? Wrong.

While my career and my leisure/passions dials and groupings were on fire, I was blowing up, repeatedly, in another area of my life – my physical health.

I broke my collarbone, for the second time, messing around with a yoga pose I had absolutely no business doing. All because I felt I should be progressing faster. Silly but not serious. The near-fatal mistake however, was not far away.

I ignored nearly three months of laboured breathing and significant weight loss just a few weeks later. When things got sufficiently bad that I couldn't finish my cycle to work without stopping to catch my breath, and clients and friends who hadn't seen me for a few weeks could not hide their shock at the disappearance of 15 per cent of my body mass, I eventually took myself to the doctor. I was then swiftly, urgently and very scarily diagnosed with multiple pulmonary embolisms, aged 30.

Pulmonary embolisms, or PEs, are blood clots in the lungs. They are nasty things. For around 25 per cent of PE sufferers, the first symptom is classed as 'sudden death'.[1] Frankly I'm not sure that death should really be described as a symptom, but there you go. On top of that, another 10–30 per cent of patients will die within a month of diagnosis.[2] All in all, this is not the kind of thing you want to get, and certainly not the kind of thing to ignore for months. The fact that I did, while getting deep into all things yoga – a meditation designed for being in and aware of one's body – should be embarrassingly noted here too.

The health blow-ups didn't quite end here either, to my further shame. Thanks to the invention of a wonderful new batch of blood-thinning medication, the treatment for my PEs was remarkably light touch: a pill a day for six months which resolved the clots, and in turn gave my damaged lungs and heart time to recover. However, I failed to recognise what damage the weight loss had wreaked on my body.

A few pounds crept back on, but as the heavy-duty blood thinners stopped me from safely doing my cycle commute, I threw myself into more and more yoga – practising at least once a day, often more once I'd added in a class. I did my yoga teacher-training in an intense three-and-a-bit weeks and started teaching too. So skinny I started, and even skinnier I stayed. Which looked great on Instagram (ugh, yes, this is absolutely the downside of social media and growing up a nineties child), but not so great when it came to trying to get pregnant.

Hunting for the cause of the PEs had sent my doctors on a mission. They ultimately discovered I have a genetic blood-clotting disorder which meant I should never have been on the combined oral contraceptive I had been taking for years. But en route to that, they first wanted to rule out cancer, which clots are often a symptom of. Which they did, thank goodness. But along the way they found polycystic ovaries. So, when we'd got through the six-month blood-thinning treatment which delayed our original 'stop trying not to get pregnant' plans and no periods returned, it was a quick hop-step to blaming ovaries and starting down a fertility treatment path.

Fortunately, as those early drugs-based attempts failed, and more extreme procedures began to be suggested (including one with the particularly horrific name of 'ovarian drilling'), my husband and I sought a second opinion. That specialist listened – really listened – to the whole story and told me to put on some weight. Which I did.

A year after the PE diagnosis, I was pregnant with my first son.

Whooooof. I'm going to pause here with the health drama and bring us back to the start of this chapter: I was getting a lot done, but I was absolutely blowing up too. And it is only by the grace of who-knows-what that those blow-ups were recoverable from.

I had all the things I wanted in my life – my dials were right there: right job, right partner, a hobby I loved in yoga and one that brought true meditation and spirituality to my life for the first time, all the fun that a large social media community can bring (it's not all be-skinny pressures, promise), trips to see the world and the financial stability to afford fertility treatment and privately-paid-for second opinions. My dashboard was spot-on:

the life I thought I wanted to live was making me so happy, and building towards the future I wanted.

But I was hurting my body again and again. This is when I started to realise that I was missing a crucial piece of the puzzle.

DIALLING UP AND DIALLING DOWN

Part three of The Dials framework is the levels. This is the verb part – the action, the doing: dialling it up and dialling it down to get the levels right on your dials. Dials are designed to be adjusted. You can think of this as a number from 1 to 10, or as a low/medium/high setting; whatever makes it manageable and meaningful for you.

We cannot be 100 per cent on in every component of our lives at every moment. Even when it feels like we are getting away with it, the cost is clocking up somewhere.

Your dials are meant to be dialled up and dialled down, depending on your needs, your wants and whatever else life is throwing at you. Let me say it again, you cannot be 100 per cent on every component, every dial, of your life at the same time. If you don't set the levels on your dials, they will get set for you. Often in ways you do not like.

Some people will interpret this as saying that 'you can't have it all' or that 'you can have it all, but not at the same time'. I refute both approaches. Again, language shapes experience.

Your dashboard is about working out what 'it all' means for you.

Your dials are about what you 'have' – what is actually in your life.

The levels at which your dials are set is how we reframe the 'not at the same time' piece and bin the 'not at all' one.

'Not at the same time' harks back to everything that is wrong with 'work–life balance': that there is an immediate, direct and discrete exchange. That you must have one, then the other. 'Can't have it all' tells us that if you do get more than one thing you want then it is vulnerable, teetering on an apex and destined to fall at any moment. But this is not how life works!

The days I didn't spend working on this book during the depths of the third national lockdown while pregnant, shielding, working full-time and managing a toddler with no childcare didn't make 'the book' any less real to me. It didn't cease to exist because the time to work on it did. Time passed, the COVID threat waned, vaccines arrived, my nanny returned, the baby was born and eventually started sleeping long enough for me to open my laptop again. My investment banking career didn't vanish during the six or so months I was on maternity leave. My relationship with my best friend is no less present for me because we are both knee-deep in nappies and don't currently have the time to do the long lunches and chill days that we used to indulge in.

You will already be adjusting your dials daily: we are all generally forced to do this via the pressures of a seven-day week. 'Work' is higher intensity during the week than, hopefully, at the weekends, while a 'kids' dial will often be the inverse. It can be a helpful tool to think about your dials on this very short time frame, but I find zooming out slightly to think about 'the now' as a season of your life is even more helpful.

IDENTIFYING THE SEASONS OF LIFE

A season is a term which is deliberately flexible. The season of utter chaos that comes with parenting small kids is a few (long!) years. The season of going for a big promotion at work could be 18 months. The season of training for a marathon might be four months. A season of caring for your beloved family member who is battling an illness could be indeterminate. A season of extra evening shifts to pay off your credit card debt is one thing; a season of working extreme hours to bed in a new career is another. A season of travelling the world post-retirement sounds pretty good too.

Setting and adjusting the levels on your dials boils down to these questions: in this season of life, what is important *and* what is possible?

Ola

When my fiancé's mum was diagnosed with cancer, everything else in my life stopped. All there was left was looking after him, his mum and my work. They both needed me. But I lost something in it all. I lost who I was because I turned everything else off. To be honest, when I look back, I realise it was a real mental health issue for me. It's taken me a few years to come back from it and, while I don't regret anything – they both needed me and I was so glad to be able to be there for them – I realise what a hard season of life that was . . . so hard, and everything else just got turned down.

The important

Thinking back to those few years when I stormed ahead with everything except my health, aside from embarrassment and extreme amounts of gratitude, the feeling that lingers is mild incredulity. Not that any of it happened, but that I could still have stormed ahead with everything *and* looked after my health. The tweaks I would have had to make then were just that – tweaks. Dialling down the 'everything else' to a 9 rather than 10 out of 10 would have given me more than enough time and space to pay proper attention to my health. Yet I didn't do it. I confused what was urgent for what was important.

> **Questions to ask yourself**
> - Can you think of a time when you found yourself pouring effort and energy into one thing, while something much more precious was put aside?
> - What is the easiest component part of life for you to drop when life gets hectic?
> - What are some of the component parts of life which give you more energy when you spend time on them?
>
> _____
>
> _____
>
> _____
>
> _____

Health, when it is as stark as it was for me, is an easy one to label as important. But the truth is that it gets cloudier and cloudier the further we move away from the acute life versus death distinctions. Ultimately, we all know we should be exercising and eating right and maintaining relationships and hobbies that keep us happy, because these are the route to a long and content life.

Yet we are, whether we like it or not, in the business of playing probabilities. The likelihood is that most of us will make it to old age: life expectancy is what it is precisely because it is the average age that people live to. That's 83 years in Spain, 85 in Japan, or a little less for Americans and Brits: 78.9 and 81.3 respectively.[3] That is a whole lot of life for most of us to fill.

The conundrum we must solve is thus: managing the short-term versus long-term trades that a near-100-year life generates. Ultimately, nothing is more important than your health – physical and mental – or the relationships that sustain you.

Yet, as we live those 70, 80, 90 or more years there are going to be opportunities and challenges that come our way at specific moments. There are going to be foundations of a fulfilled life that we have a better chance to build at a particular moment in time. From the broad – financial, emotional, physical – to the narrow – that exact job, that exact house, that exact road trip across Europe with that exact group of friends. This is what truly gets lost in all the talk of work–life balance and having or not having 'it all'.

Important looks like this: it is important to dial down most things and run, hard, at that once-in-a lifetime opportunity. **There will be things that can only be done in this season of your life. So, do them.** Explicitly and deliberately throw balance to the frickin' kerb and go go go on that thing that is important to you. This could be work, or personal, or travel, or something else entirely. Whatever 'it' is should be right there on your dashboard. For me, first it was children and then it was a big career goal.

> **Dev**
> *I've been on the senior leadership team at my organisation for years and I've just stepped up to acting director. The board are interviewing for a permanent hire, and I am going through that process too. This is a once-in-a-lifetime opportunity for me. I love this place: I've spent most of my career here and think I can make a real difference to the organisation and the cause from that top spot. It's not that I need to drop everything else or turn it all to zero, but this is coming first for the foreseeable future.*

I paused the story earlier in this chapter at the point when I was pregnant for the first time after a rollercoaster ride to get there.

I was indescribably happy and I knew that I wanted to savour every moment of the pregnancy and my maternity leave, because I also knew that I wanted, and needed, to go back to work – a desire that was clarified as again and again people, both in and out of the world of my work, hinted or just came right out and said that motherhood would 'change me'. That I might not want to 'only' take the industry-leading six months full pay my company offered. That I might not want to return full-time, or care as much about the promotion once I gave birth. Just as that career coach had assumed.

This concept that the moment you become a 'mother' you are an entirely new person is inescapable as a woman. It is sprinkled gently but consistently through popular culture and then often rammed down our throats too. A transmogrified version of English essayist Cyril Connolly's statement that 'there is no more sombre enemy of good art than the pram in the hall'[4] – written in 1938 but living strong in the 39 million results that appear once you type in the question 'Does motherhood change you?' into your internet browser. (Note, a similar search with the word 'fatherhood' in it garners fewer than 20 per cent of the same volume of results.)

Then the baby came. With his wild blonde hair and bright blue eyes. With his personality shining through from day one: watchful, initially cautious, but then all-in with a fierce and focused determination that made me realise, quickly and slightly to my horror, that this apple had not fallen far from my tree.

And in some ways, I was changed. A new love opened – for him, for my husband and for the amazing things my body could do. And the science confirms that there are some observable changes: various studies show that neural networks reprogram for new parents, specifically the ones linked to emotional processing, social understanding and cognitive empathy, but – spoiler – that this happens the same for mothers and for fathers; the variable is not sex or gender, but the amount of time caring for the child.[5,6]

Still, I waited. I waited for the other penny to drop. For the desire to achieve the things I knew I was capable of, the ambition to build the life I wanted for my family in those years 'BC' (Before Children) to change, like so many people, and the patriarchy, either told me or insinuated it would.

Tumbleweed.

It didn't.

I breathed a sigh of relief.

I was still me. I still wanted the things I wanted before: a happy marriage, the chance to raise my own children and enjoy that process, professional success, the earning power to build the kind of life I wanted for me and for my family and the choices that money affords. All the things that were on my dashboard 'BC'.

I wanted to dial the world of work right down while I nestled into the baby bubble and recovered from the pregnancy and birth. Which I did. I threw myself headfirst into new parenthood, taking six and a bit months off, four of which my husband was off alongside me (shared parental leave being the wonder invention of the 2010s). I loved it. The milky cuddles, the milestones, the long walks with him strapped to me, gurgling away, the longer nights getting up again and again to feed him knowing that the tiredness didn't really matter because all I had to do the next day was more milky cuddles and long walks.

And then, while my husband did an additional two months of paternity leave solo, I went back to work. I went back to get that damn promotion.

And just like that, the work dial that had been turned right down, even all the way down, was ramped up to full blast. The kids dial which had been the one on my dashboard on the highest setting was taken down a few notches – even several notches for those months while my husband was home, before it crept back up to a steadier state once he too went back to work and we both dashed home at the end of the day for playtime, bath time and bedtime.

I had two opportunities in front of me: a promotion and precious time with my first child. The promotion was the one that would make a meaningful difference to the money I was earning then and there, my future earning potential and therefore both the kind of life we could live and the freedom of choice available to us. It was the one that would validate all the extreme hours and tough, tough moments in my early twenties. It was the one that would open doors to more responsibility and roles that would be even more fun for me to do every day. And the baby was the one that spoke to the 'build a family' part of my dashboard.

I could have delayed one or the other, potentially. Having it all, just not at the same time, though there were no guarantees either would be waiting indefinitely down the track for me.

Instead, on these two occasions at least, I prioritised the important. And I did it by getting the levels right on my dials at the precise moments the seasons of my life afforded me the opportunity. I dialled each up and down when it mattered to get where I wanted to be.

I got want I wanted and, this time, I did it without blowing myself up.

Questions to ask yourself

- What is the one – yes, just one – thing which you would choose this year to be about if you had to decide? What about the next five years?
- What is unique about the season of life you are in now and what you can do with the opportunities around or ahead of you?
- Is there a recurring hurdle that trips you up in life? How have you avoided it or gracefully leaped over it before? How can you build more of that into life next time it is needed?

_____

_____

_____

_____

The possible

'Important', however, is only part of the puzzle.

I can toot my own horn all day about how smart and wise I was to dial up family on maternity leave and dial up work heading into a promotion. Except I didn't do it all by myself. And it didn't happen because I am magically so smart and wise. At all.

Being able to go back to work with the level of support I had was a true privilege made up of many, many components. From a husband who cared enough to take the time off and dial down his career in the same way I did, to affording the kind of dedicated and flexible childcare that meant we could both go back to our demanding jobs post eight months of shared parental leave. It meant we didn't have to stress too much about running out of the office if something important came up, and the luxuries of coming home to the baby's laundry being done and home-cooked food being stacked up in the freezer.

On top of all that, I had a huge level of support, sponsorship, mentorship and friendship from colleagues, bosses and clients while pregnant and once I went back to the office. This is something that is missing for scores and scores of pregnant women and mothers. The Equality and Human Rights Commission in the UK estimates that 54,000 women are pushed out of their jobs due to pregnancy and maternity related discrimination and disadvantage a year, and that 77 per cent of working mothers have encountered negative or discriminatory treatment at work.[7] The year I worked the fewest hours in my career in investment banking was the year I returned from maternity leave and made MD. Yes, 11 years of working my socks off to get to that point stood me in massively good stead. But that would have been insufficient if I hadn't had the right people around me, coaching and supporting me to spend my – now more limited – time well and ensure that my work dial was turned right up on the things that would really make a professional difference. Each piece was an essential part of making what was important, possible.

These contributory factors, however, are ones that not everyone, unfortunately, has available to them. Yes, I learned important lessons in the previous years and then implemented them. But the 24 hours I now have in my day are not the same as the ones I had in my early twenties: I have amassed more control, more support, more wealth, all of which quite literally afford me more time.

And the 24 hours I will have available to me in a month or a year or 10 are likely to be different again: more or less resource, more or less health, more or less of all sorts of things. Which is precisely the reason why having a dynamic, intentional framework with which to approach life is so valuable.

What is possible is going to reflect several things: the bigger picture realities of our personal histories, the immediate resources we do or do not have at our disposal, the reality of this season of each of our lives, and what is in our control and what is not.

Sometimes the levels on our dials get set for us. The COVID pandemic painted this in harsh detail. Women's jobs were 1.8 times more vulnerable than men's jobs. Women make up 39 per cent of global employment but accounted for 54 per cent of overall job losses. One reason for this greater effect on women is that when family members fall ill and schools close, those who already pick up more of the unpaid care burden – women – take on those extra responsibilities. Women's employment through the pandemic dropped faster than average, even accounting for the fact that women and men work in different sectors.[8] On top of this, the unjust effects of the pandemic were worse for women of colour. Black women were three times more likely than non-Black women to report the death of a loved one as a challenge to their careers during the pandemic and 43 per cent of Latinas were spending five or more hours per day on housework and caregiving, compared to only 34 per cent of women overall. Almost a third of Latinas were on 'double duty' (caring for children and an adult, such as an elderly family member) – a significant additional burden.[9]

This is just a smattering of statistics which casts light on a tiny fraction of the intersecting and compounding biases that people face in the workplace due to many aspects of identity, all of which can move things firmly out of the 'possible' category. Your family dial might get turned up for you by a massive event like a global pandemic, making any other adjustment to the levels of your dials impossible in this season of life.

While I expect the world to be haunted by the shadow of the pandemic for many decades to come, things which make dialling up or dialling down possible, or indeed impossible, aren't always going to be of this scale. Particularly when it comes to careers. There are peaks and troughs, times of lots of momentum and times of plateaus and consolidation. Many, even most, of which won't be directly in our control.

We will get into this in much more detail in Chapter 6, but the relevant point here is that sometimes you need to wait that extra year until your boss's internal transfer goes through and you get offered their role. Sometimes you need that big campaign to launch and bear fruit before you pitch your dream client. Sometimes you need to get a couple of years of sales numbers or management responsibility under your belt to be in consideration for that bigger role. Sometimes the opportunity you need just won't happen on the path you are on or in the place you are at, and you need to spend some time working out how to change paths or places to create what you are missing. Then, of course, it all takes time to do.

Chloe

I am in a work rut and it is deeply frustrating. It's not obvious to me how I am going to progress in my current role – I've done everything I feel like I can in this seat. That frustration forced me into having difficult conversations and saying what I want. I've spoken to my boss, and other managers, but no one seems to have a good solution, or any solution to be honest. I've started going to the gym more during the day, which has had a net positive effect on my life. But still, my instinct is to try to fight the fight with work. I don't want my work dial to be so low. Work is an important enough part of life that I have to take it into my control. So if this job dial is all the way down, despite me trying to turn it back up, I am changing my definition of what work is. I'm adding a 'find a new job' dial next to my 'current job' dial. And that is the one I'm turning all the way up.

The thing that might feel the most important might not be possible for several reasons. Thankfully, though, thinking on what is not possible can often reveal something else that is.

I was (hell, still very much can be) impatient, grumbling about why I can't move faster, do more, now now now. But it was in one of these periods when it wasn't possible to turn up the 'work at my current job' dial that allowed me to turn up another dial which would become central to my life: my yoga dial.

I was a year or so into moving across into the nascent relationship management team, 'nascent' being the operative word here. We were a new team, doing a new function and I was totally new not only to the role itself, but to many of the products, colleagues and clients I was dealing with every day. I had huge amounts to learn. And we had lots of people to persuade.

This was a different pace to the frenetic and constant world of FX sales trading. For the first time in my career, I wasn't tied to every news headline hitting the wires, or data point being announced, or tick of a price movement on the tapes. And it felt strange. Exacerbated by the fact that I enjoyed it all so much more. Bringing people together, scoping out solutions, iterating them with experts, having my assumptions challenged, changing people's minds, getting up to speed quickly on an entirely new corners of financial markets: this was *fun*.

I know now that this was because I was, for the first time, in the right job for me. Yet it felt odd. It felt like I wasn't working hard enough. Because it wasn't hard. Sure, I had bad days, even weeks. Multi-month run-ins with one or two particularly difficult people which sometimes led to tears-in-the-toilet-cubicle moments. I made mistakes; technical ones in front of senior people, miscalculations about how to play a particular scenario with a client, forgetting to tell someone important something and telling too much to someone else. But still, the worst parts of this job only made me want to be better at it. And the best parts, well, did I tell you before that it was fun?

But rather than simply enjoying it, I felt like I needed to push even more. Doing something that suited my skills, my temperament and that I excelled at left me with a bunch of emotional, physical and psychic energy that I needed to allocate somewhere. And given my 'work at my current job' dial had always consumed every piece of all those things, it had to be allocated there. Right?

Wrong. Because I had the new job, the big opportunity. I was already working hard and taking on responsibility ahead of my age and stage. I didn't need to 'do more' – I just needed to do what I was doing already.

Two fortuitous things happened around this time. A couple of colleagues sat me down and told me, frankly, to calm down. And I started yoga.

Over the next few months, almost unwittingly to begin with, I took a couple of intensity points off my 'work at my current job' dial and shifted them over to a new dial on my dashboard: yoga.

All the burning impatience I had which I thought needed to be channelled into work, initially found another home: keeping me on a yoga mat, even when it felt so impossible to stick with (clearly there is no way 'Downward Dog' is a resting pose! How are all these people touching their toes? Wait, what . . . you are meant to pause in that half-push-up shape . . . *for a whole breath?*).

And as months, and eventually years, passed, all that time on my mat in a moving meditation and consistent practice of small failure (how is it that I still fall out of triangle pose?), cultivated a deeper patience for life in general. It taught me that I could put my energy into things other than work (babies, yoga, book-writing, community-building) and still be excellent at my job. That it would help me to be better at managing some of the impatience that got me to where I am in my career in the first place.

So much of using the levels on your dials is about being intentional: in the best of circumstances, like having a great new job to get stuck into, but one that needs some time; or tricky circumstances, like navigating a health scare; or even in the worst of circumstances – when catastrophe strikes, many other things in life must wait. There is a huge amount of power, and freedom, to be found in the dialling up and the dialling down.

Emily

The next six to nine months are all about work and the house move (we've just had an offer accepted on our first property). Those are the two dials that are way up. My business partner is going on maternity leave soon, and we have several amazing projects on the go. There is a lot to do and I finally have the capacity to dig in on it all, which is so exciting.

What is getting turned down slightly is my son – he is in a really great place, settled in at his new senior school, and he just doesn't need me quite as much as he did in the last few years. And our dogs. I know this sounds silly, but they were intense for a period there! Well, they still are. But my partner is spending more time with them now as his work is also a bit quieter until his next big project launches at the end of the year. So, in short, it's on him to train the new puppy.

Things that aren't changing are the gym – I get up at 5am so I can go to a gym class before my son wakes up. And while I'd love to do more competitions and other classes, this is fine for life right now. Well, probably the next few years.

> *Family time with my partner and son is not quite where I'd like it to be. We end up doing a lot of stuff separately as it's the only way to get it all done. It won't be like this forever. But it's something I need to keep an eye on and maybe talk through with them both.*

Levels prompts
- What season of life are you in?
- What is important right now?
- What is possible currently, in your specific circumstances?
- Linking back to your dashboard, which of your priorities/pillars of your life can be built on best now?

SETTING YOUR LEVELS

Step 1: Get your dials back in front of you
Jot down next to each of your dials roughly how much of your time/energy each is taking. This can be numeric (a scale of 1–5 or 1–10), or simply high/medium/low.

Step 2: Critically review your dials
- Are you happy with these levels?
- Are you spending time where you want to?
- Do your high/medium/lows reflect what is important right now?
- Do your high/medium/lows reflect what is possible right now?
- Are you at or near breaking point? Are you bored and uninspired? Where needs more, or less, energy?
- Look back against your dashboard: are the levels you have set reflective of the values, goals and priorities that are on your dashboard?

Step 3: Adjust the level
- What needs to get dialled up, or down?
- Right now, or soon?

Your levels recap

Dials are designed to be adjusted. We cannot be 100 per cent 'on' in every component of our lives at every moment. Even when it feels like we are getting away with it, the price will always be getting paid in another area of our lives.

We need to consciously assess what level each of our dials is set to. This is deliberately and intentionally about life right now. What needs more, what needs less? Where is it possible to be more 'in', where might it not be?

But the very nature of a dial – something designed to be adjusted – speaks to usability, which is that you are going to be changing the settings on these dials – dialling up or dialling down – as life, needs, opportunities and capacity change. What is important to us, and what is possible right now.

Chapter 5

BUILDING FOR RESILIENCE

THE FIRST THREE steps in The Dials framework are extremely concrete – seductively so. You can decide who you are and what kind of life you want to live (your dashboard). You can choose what components your life is represented by (your dials). You can intentionally set the intensity of energy or time you are putting into those components in any given season of your life (your levels). Bish bash bosh; job done. Right?

Except, we all know that a *huge* part of life is totally uncontrollable. Change is coming whether you want it to or not. Order is temporary. Certainty is short-lived. It is not that uncertainty or change are just a part or a feature of the system. They are the *very essence* of it.

If we let ourselves either forget that or, worse, fight against it, we are in for trouble. Nassim Nicholas Taleb in his book *Antifragile* tells us that 'it is far easier to figure out if something is fragile than to predict the occurrence of an event that may harm it'.[1] The truth here is that it doesn't even take much figuring out to know that we, and our lives, and our plans for them, are fragile. And we can't predict what specific event is going to come along and change everything: we just know it is going to happen at some point.

So, what to do?

The fourth, and final, part of The Dials framework is about building resilience at every opportunity. About making sure each of the first three steps can withstand and recover, when, frankly, shit happens. And that you are, deliberately and intentionally, prioritising resilience as you build and operate each part of your Dials. It looks like this:

(Dashboard | Dials | Levels) ^{Resilience}

Resilience is not a step in and of itself, but a consistent reflection, a lens through which to see the other steps. It is a consideration time and time again as you make big decisions: this job or that job; this place or that place; this person or that person; yes or no, as you assess the path you are already on.

Resilience isn't universally definable or something you achieve and then are done with. I can no more specify it for myself than decide what it looks like for you. But whatever 'it' is for each of us, it is *extremely* important. It is not just an exact amount of money, or a particular fallback, or a magic number of people in our lives, or an indefatigable sense of self. It can be all those things and none of them for every single one of us.

You will know you are getting this resilience factor right when you have more control to take dials on and off your dashboard, when you have more control to adjust the levels of those dials and when your dashboard is so clear to you that you can live true to yourself and your ideals even in the shittiest of circumstances.

This control will never be total. The universe will still decide to whack on a new dial for you or turn two up to max when you didn't want that to happen – and sometimes do both of those things simultaneously. Just because. A loved one gets diagnosed with an illness, a water pipe bursts and floods your flat, a crisis happens at work . . . But when that happens – and it is 'when', not 'if' – more resilience in your life will mean you can dial down something else or add/remove other dials to make life more manageable. Or you can take some comfort in the fact that this moment of intensity is temporary; knowing that the life you have built, are building, is so honest to you and your priorities that it can withstand the whirlwind for a time.

We can't control everything in life. Yet if we aim for resilience, we should be able to control some things, even in the wildest and most uncertain times.

Questions to ask yourself

- Are you heading in a direction that will have flex if, though more likely when, things change?
- Are the choices you are making, the wants you are describing, overly prescriptive?
- Does spending more time on this part of your life get you greater or fewer options down the road?

_____

_____

_____

_____

DASHBOARD RESILIENCE

A couple of years ago, my first son went through 'The Dinosaur Phase' – a period of toddlerhood some young kids experience with a ferocity that only a T-Rex can understand. In the middle of it, I read him book after book after book on all things dinosaurs. I responded to endless questions about this type of creature and that period of time, most of which I only knew the answers to by surreptitiously asking Google. It is impossible to walk alongside a little person during this phase and not be repeatedly reminded of just how short human existence on this planet is.

This sense of time, of perspective, was – is – only slightly less incomprehensible to me than it was to him. The reality that all the things that loom so large in our own lives and even the generations of our own family's lives are just the tiniest fraction of reality. And with it all, the appreciation of a wild and long series of events which trace these words being written all the way back in time to those dinosaurs that many tiny people are fascinated with.

There are already a truly unfathomable number of paths behind each of us. And even more potential paths ahead depending on many factors in our control: who we kiss, who we work for, whether we get the train or drive to tomorrow's destination. And many which are not. But still, truly millions. Billions. Perhaps even trillions.

Yet, if I tried to optimise for a very specific outcome – just one of those paths on the tree of possibilities ahead – then it wouldn't take much to knock me off course. I might end up on the path right next door to the one I had dreamed of – an imperceptible difference to anyone else, but that miss could feel massively significant to me. If I have hung my fulfilment hat on landing on one *precise* version of life, then the disappointment of not getting there could be devastating.

I have got this wrong so many times – the mortgage-free by 30 goal I told you about in Chapter 2 being a prime example. It was a 'goal' that betrayed a stunning level of ignorance about my earning capacity, the cost of London housing and what life would look like for me some 10+ years later (where

I would be working and where my family would be living, just to name a couple of important factors). My obsession with getting promoted to Managing Director before I became a mother was another example. It was a 'goal' that meant I put so much pressure on myself that I failed to do my best at work and therefore delayed the very promotion I was so fixated on.

By being far, far too prescriptive, I made my goals, and ultimately my enjoyment of life, vulnerable. I could never control those specific things. Ever. But I created the sense of failure and pressure and expectation that never needed to exist.

Lamenting the gap between what popular culture thought 'the future' would bring and the reality, entrepreneur Peter Thiel made the slogan of his venture capital firm, 'we wanted flying cars, instead we got 140 characters' – a pithy comment on the *Back to the Future* movies of the eighties and the version of 2015 that was actually delivered, featuring Twitter.[2] And, yes, if the only version of 'cool stuff in the future' Thiel would have been happy with was non-ground-based vehicles, then it is easy to see the disappointment. Yet if Thiel had been hoping for human innovation in a broader sense, then it is hard to look around and not see stunning examples. Like, CRISPR gene editing hailing the beginning of the end of horrific genetic diseases. Or 4G making access to the internet truly available on the go.

The key here is to give your dashboard the resilience of breadth. To capture enough of what is important to you, but not to be so specific that anything that fails to perfectly match it is a failure.

Questions to ask yourself
- Can you think of a time when you were holding on to a specific version of the future and then were disappointed when it didn't come to pass in the *exact* format you were hoping for?
- What about an example where, perhaps with hindsight, you got what you wanted but didn't recognise it at the time?

_____

_____

_____

_____

Our dashboards are about who we are and what matters to us. They are an explicit expression of the kind of life we want to live, what we want to achieve and how we want our lives to be. And this is how we make them resilient in a world where anything can happen – truly anything. We articulate versions of all those things which are as broad as possible but still capture our personal truths, our values and priorities – like sketching out the goal of a loving family unit, rather than specifying that this must be in the exact format of a long-standing marriage and two children; or prioritising professional success, rather than spelling out that this means a precise promotion level, or client acquired, or number of books sold. This way, we can find fulfilment in multiple paths.

The more we have breadth on our dashboards, the more we are building in resilience against everything the world can, will and does throw at us.

Knowing your why

In the examples of the two (very specific) goals I set for myself, which we discussed earlier in the chapter, there was a golden kernel of something that was true to me and what I wanted – needed – on my dashboard. The mortgage or lack thereof was about a place to call home and a protected, safe space to raise a family – something that loomed large for me as the daughter of a military father who had lived in 13 houses by the age of 18 and went to boarding school aged 7. Promotion-before-babies was about being in a place in my career where I would have some control over the hours I worked and having the opportunity to enjoy the early hectic years of parenthood rather than simply fighting to get through them. For in the mistakes I made on overspecifying the things that were important to me, I was homing in on another way to build resilience into my dreams.

If you know *why* you are working or loving or learning, especially those times when you have no frickin' clue whether what you are doing is even half right, then every 'failure' is just as valuable as every 'success'. Because now you have real-life data points. Ones which tell you whether the choices you are making reflect what is important to you. And those are *massively* valuable even if the 'thing' itself – the new hobby, job, lover – didn't work out so well. This is why something that can seem like, and very much feel like, a failure, does not have to be so. It might not be what you first intended, but the lessons you learn from it and the data you collect from it can be invaluable guidance.

Knowing your 'why' will enable you to set sufficiently broad goals that they can be achievable in multiple ways.

It's so easy to look at someone else's life and think they have it all worked out. To see the successes and think they planned the steps and flawlessly executed them to reach their goals in a beautiful, straight, smooth upwards line. The never-ending social media highlight reel is a massive contributor to that.

Surely this is exactly how it worked for Michael Phelps, the most decorated Olympian of all time. Right? You train, you win, you train more, you win more, until you are the best. Except, no.

Phelps battled depression and suicidal thoughts during his entire swimming career. The pursuit of becoming the best swimmer in the world was, he has described, so brutal, so relentless, that he closed off every other part of himself until he came to the point where he 'was just a swimmer, and not a human being'.[3]

Despite his success, Phelps' goals were too specific to bring him happiness: he didn't understand what really mattered to him, and how to be a human being rather than 'just' being the best swimmer who had ever lived. Even gold medals and being acclaimed the world over is not enough when there isn't a meaningful enough *why* behind it all.

This a classic teaching of the philosopher Nietzsche ('He who has a why to live can bear almost any how'), and one we should take forward when we think about making our dashboards as resilient as possible.[4]

Think or refer back to what started to come out for you in the dashboard chapter. Are there any goals on there that are hyper-specific or overly prescriptive? Anything that, when you review it now, gives you a little shiver of fear that if it doesn't come about in the exact way you are envisioning you might be disappointed? This is the moment to tweak it, to reframe it to something a bit broader. Be kinder to yourself and your future – give it the space to be what it can, and will, be and be grateful for *that*, not disappointed because it wasn't exactly what you thought it would be.

Hannah

A key piece of my dashboard is about wanting to collect stories and experiences rather than stuff. It is why I joined the military, and a piece of why I left after a decade. I knew that I had got the experiences I wanted from it but didn't have a specific idea of what was going to come next. It took me the next few years to work out that I find my knowing through not knowing.

A big dashboard value for me is living a life where I can respect that process of trying things and then working out through experience what is and is not for me – where that trial and error is OK. I know now I am never going to have these precise life goals that many other people seem to have. I'm not about building towards a goal. There is something sculptors say about their work: that they are chipping away the stone that doesn't look like the piece. That is how I think about it. And that is the value, the approach, I need to keep expressing on my dashboard and through my dials.

DIALS RESILIENCE

The dials on your dashboard are the component parts of your life: the how and what of how you spend your time – physically, mentally and emotionally. And damn straight, we need all this to be as hard as nails, while also able to bend and not break – to be resilient.

Baking resilience into your dials is about considering a set of dials which contain all the things that make life today worth living *and* the things that will keep you going way way way (please!) into the future: health, relationships, fun, creativity, laughs, exercise, nature, nutrition, sex, friendships, sleep, mobility. Hell, my favourite one of these is simply, but sometimes impossibly, *rest*.

Dials that help you stay the course

Clemency Burton-Hill says she is an 'abject failure' at resting.[5] As a former BBC Young Musician of the Year (a violinist), an author, a journalist, a broadcaster and a mother of two, Clemency thrived on living life at an astounding pace, cramming as much into every day as possible – going to music bars after dinners with friends to inhale a jazz performance, waking up early to see an art exhibition before work. More was always more. She was at the top of her game when, aged 39, she suffered a massive brain haemorrhage: a malformed set of blood vessels in her head that had existed since she was born exploded, destroying the left side of her brain, a scale of injury very few people survive.

Luckily, Clemency was in central New York with the best brain surgeons and neurologists on hand and she became the exception. However, the road to recovery from a brain injury of that nature is long, slow and arduous and it centres especially around, you guessed it, rest. Rest, Clemency's neurologists tell her, is what gives the brain time to forge new neural pathways and connections to replace what was lost and damaged: to speak, walk, live again. Yet 'rest is so difficult for me,' she says, 'I have no muscle memory' of it. So, on top of all the 'old' skills she has to relearn, Clemency is learning and acquiring an entirely new skill. Which itself is hard, and exhausting.

Clearly these are rare and exceptional circumstances, but it is often these moments of crisis that show us the need to slow down, to take care of our bodies and our relationships. And how much better would it be to have made at least a little progress on this front before the crunch moment when we need it most? I say this as someone who discovered the need to prioritise rest only through having neglected it for far too long.

It's either cheesy or lazy, or possibly both, to say at this point that life is a marathon not a sprint. And if you, like me, have a visceral hatred of running, the thought of lungs and thighs burning from here to the end of your days may also fill you with both horror and yearning for a squishy sofa. But still, it's one of those things we blurt out to each other in moments of need because it rings true. Writer Alex Soojung-Kim Pang in his book *Rest*, describes rest itself as a partner to work rather than a competitor – a wonderful reframing.[6]

So much of the value of life and the things we care about in it come from just *being here* to experience it all in an enjoyable way, for as long as possible – a strong body, a happy mind, a chance to see and hear and touch the people we love as regularly as possible.

These things matter because they are brilliant in every moment they happen. And because they are the very things that are going to keep you in the game longer too. The things that mean you can stay the course when others are falling by the wayside are significantly undervalued in our current culture. Yes, rest. Yes, sleep. Yes, sex and comedy and art and hobbies that are for joy and not monetisation. Adventure. Discovery. Bad romance novels, long walks and Wordle WhatsApp groups.

Even if these things feel impossible, I urge you to put them on your dials.

A dial can exist on your dashboard for a long time and be set at zero. I hope that your nature or your rest dials will never

ever find that setting, but there are times when some things just aren't – can't be – set to max. And that is OK. But there is real value to having one or two, or more, of these dials on there no matter what.

As we talked about in Chapter 4, there are, will always be, seasons of life when some things take up so much time and energy that other things must wait. The sci-fi novel draft collects dust. Naps go out of the window. Dinners with friends become fewer and further between. But that novel, those naps, these friends are still important to you. And keeping your writing dial, or your mid-afternoon snooze dial, or your friends-from-university dial right there on your dashboard is an important pledge to yourself. That one day, tomorrow we hope, you will get back to them.

Lily

This is my 'selfish' dial. One day, it will be travelling the world once the kids are off and out of the house living their own lives. For now, it's going out for dinner just the two of us every now and again – though that has been turned down a lot over the last few months while I sorted this new job and the kids moved schools. But it's there. And I'm now thinking about when and how I need to turn it up a bit more.

LEVELS RESILIENCE

Setting the levels on your dials is an inherently resilient act – one of prioritisation, one of acknowledgement: of the amount of time and energy you have and where it matters or is possible for you to spend it. A statement of truth, to yourself and the world, that there are only 24 hours in every day and that those 24 are still often woefully insufficient to do all the things we need, or would like, to get done.

Yet the fight about those 24 hours rages on. There are the purists who argue the technicalities. Of course, the maths is that a day is the same duration for each of us. They point to the many examples of people who have overcome incredible hardship and challenges to do extraordinary things. And then there are those on the other end of the spectrum who argue it is a lot more complicated – a camp I am firmly bedded down in. The 24 hours I have in my day now are not the same as the 24 that someone who is responsible for a chronically ill relative gets. Or someone who lives in a country with less generous paid parental leave. Or someone who doesn't have the safety net of friends and family around them. Or who is disabled; so, the 40 minutes it takes me to get up and out of the door takes them 3 hours.

Crikey, whenever anyone tells the story of Steve Jobs or Barack Obama wearing the same clothes every day in order to focus their mental capacity on other areas of their lives, I am reminded that the rules just don't apply to everyone in the same way. In a world where women are judged much more harshly on how they present themselves, it is a brave one who tries this trick on the world stage, or even on a more local one.

Go for support

We all know it is a brutal world out there. The rules are not the same for everyone, the starting points are not fair, justice is not visited on those who deserve it most. Many of you reading these words will have much harsher experiences of this than I have had or, frankly, ever will. The Dials, as useful and practical a framework as I hope it can be, cannot be the magic wand to fix all of this (though we are going to get stuck into ways you can have real impact on the things that matter later in the book).

Yet, adjusting our dials is a practical, useful, responsive way to deal with the very real, and very different, limits each of us have on our times and our lives. **To make this third and final step of The Dials into the fully resilient and hyper-useful version of itself, we must maximise our abilities to change those levels. We need to prioritise the things that mean we can do it *more*. Whatever our own baseline is.**

Shonda Rhimes, the queen of making addictive TV drama series, points out how she and so many others would skirt the question of how much help it takes to generate the level of success and output she has reached: 'I just didn't want to say it, because no one else ever said it. Powerful famous women don't say out loud that they have help at home, that they have nannies, housekeepers, chefs, assistants, stylists – whatever it is they have to keep their worlds spinning – because they are ashamed. Or maybe a more precise way to say it is that these women have *beeh shamed.*'[7]

I have already mentioned my nanny a few times in this book, and it feels *terrifying* every time I do – for so many reasons: that it implies I love my kids less because I don't look after them full-time; or maybe that they love me less because they are with someone else for the bulk of their weekdays; or that, God forbid, I am implicitly saying you can only have kids and 'success' if you can afford this kind of paid help. Vomit-inducing. And all this when the judgement should be solely placed on a system which has made childcare in the UK the most expensive in the world, some 30 per cent of average take-home pay.[8]

Shonda is right: I feel shame that this is what it takes, even at a level of life way below hers. Shame that I need it, and shame that not everyone who needs it has it. The only way those things change, however, is by casting light on to them. In a world that has trained us to think that we can or even should be doing only the most impressive things, and doing them by ourselves, this is a shout out for support systems.

Support is the compound interest of life. It sneaks up, slowly and quietly, until one day you realise it is silently but effectively working away for you and producing more than you ever could have imagined.

Support in your life, and control of the levels of your dials, can encompass a huge variety of things. Money absolutely can be a support system and a way to get more control over where your levels are set (much more on this in Chapter 10). It can be the policies and benefits available to us through companies, governments and organisations.

Other aspects of life make huge differences too, such as people – family, friends, partners and our wider communities. Yet, a big change in societies over the past 40 or so years – the trend towards smaller family units – makes some of this people-related support harder to come by. Average household size in OECD countries fell from 2.8 persons in the mid-eighties to 2.6 in the mid-noughties.[9] With a longer lens, in the US in 1790, average household size stood at 5.79. In 2018 it reached 2.63.[10] In Norway and Sweden single-person households now account for nearly half of all households, from being rare a century ago.[11]

Psychiatrist, neuroscientist and former director of the National Institute of Mental Health, Thomas Insel, argues that social isolation is one of the most under-discussed elements of mental illness and mental health. That loneliness is a major part of mental illness, and that community is a major part of mental health.[12] Yet many of us don't have these networks in the way societies used to.

At this point in my life, support absolutely includes excellent paid childcare. I stumbled into a situation where I can afford to draft in some of the support I need (though no amount of money can 'buy' someone who truly becomes part of the family; we can only thank our lucky stars that this is the situation we are now in with our nanny). If I had thought about it all more it might not have been such a surprise. I am, after all, a huge planner and kids were on that plan. But it is almost impossible to forecast out an earning trajectory and a housing cost trajectory and a career trajectory and a fertility trajectory with any meaningful accuracy. And I had one less variable than many in that I met and married my partner very young. Add in a 'if/when I meet the right person' variable and fuck only knows! And yes, that is the technical term.

I am simultaneously extremely grateful and totally horrified about this. Horrified because the system absolutely should not work this way (and it doesn't in other countries) and because I could so easily again stumble into a situation where I need a new kind of support, but the next time, have no ability to address it in the moment.

Support is also not just there for when things go wrong: it makes a huge difference when there's a big opportunity to run at, an adventure to go on, a risk to be taken. And having more ability to control the levels on your dials is going to help you: more support, more choices, more back-stops, more control.

This is a call to prioritise building support into your life. A nudge if you will.

Nobel prize-winning economists Cass Sunstein and Richard Thaler quite literally wrote the book on this.[13] A 'nudge', as they describe it, is 'any aspect of choice architecture that alters people's behaviours in a predictable way without forbidding any options or significantly changing their economic incentives'.

Let's say you are a head teacher at a school and you worry that the children in attendance are choosing the sweeter options on offer to have with their lunch. A nudge under Sunstein and Thaler's framework would be moving fruit to be front and centre at lunchtime. Something prescriptive and exclusionary like banning chocolate or biscuits from the school would not.

So, this is me quite literally putting the fruit and vegetables in your eyeline and the cookies back in the jar. Support is a must-have, not a nice-to-have. But it surprises me just how little the wider concept of support is discussed in the very places that many people turn to for it.

You need to build support into your life, even it feels redundant or underutilised: whether it is by living close to friends or family, or adding a rest dial, or a nap dial, or keeping your nature dial dialled up even when work is guzzling your time and energy, or marrying someone who is kind and supportive (or not marrying someone who isn't!), or seeking well-paid, reliable employment, or taking the higher paid job and saving more when finances allow.

We live in a world that tells us to do it all alone. And one which so often leaves us to bear the consequences when we learn that is impossible. **Being able to adjust your own dials is invaluable, and you are more likely to be able to do that more often when you have support in your life.** These things are essential pieces of how to make you, your life and your enjoyment of it, resilient.

BUILDING RESILIENCE

I want you to spend a little bit of time here thinking about how you can build resilience into your framework. Let's reflect back on what we've learned in this chapter and use the prompts to help you.

Dashboard resilience is about knowing what your why is – your purpose behind the 'what's and 'how's of spending your time. It is about thinking broadly, and not overly prescriptively, about the many versions of a future where you could be thriving, and happy, and fulfilled.

Dials resilience is a reminder to create space in your life for the things that will allow you to stay in the game – a strong body, a happy mind, a chance to see and hear and touch the people you love as regularly as possible.

Levels resilience is all about pay-offs and the power of building, of prioritising, support systems. Support systems enable you to maximise your ability to change the levels on your dials, at your time and at your choosing. That power, that responsiveness, is itself so freeing. None of us can protect ourselves from all of the extremes that life will throw at us, but if we have more support along the way, the experience of living through those tough times will be a little less fraught than otherwise.

Resilience prompts

- Dashboard check: am I being too prescriptive in my goals or priorities?
- Dials check: do I have dials that help me stay in the game? Which ones? What could I add if not?
- Levels check: how am I building support systems into my life? What does that look like now, and in the future?

Your resilience recap

Resilience matters in all its forms. This will manifest in the ability, the opportunity, to both choose what dials you have on your dashboard *and* the level at which those dials are set more frequently. Not all the time. Not always, but more often than otherwise.

That control itself has massive value. Even when it is also true that uncertainty and change are intrinsic to the system we all operate in. This final piece of the framework reminds us all to acknowledge this truth and work with it, rather than fight it.

Part 2

THE DIALS IN THE REAL WORLD

Chapter 6

WHY QUITTING ISN'T (IMMEDIATELY) THE ANSWER

'YOURS IS "quick and dirty".'

Wowzers. There dropped a little conversational bomb. I blushed. My brain whirred, and lacked, for a witty response.

My small team and I were out for a get-together and I'd stepped away from the group to get in the next round of drinks. A kind bartender offered to bring them across to us, so I popped back much quicker than expected and caught the end of a conversation between our three endlessly patient, hard-working and energetic analysts/associates. Each worked closely with one of the senior relationship managers on the team and they were comparing our relative approaches to the job, boiling us down to one oft- and over-used phrase.

We had 'that's proper' from one of us who was fond of empha-sising good work, good restaurants and good jokes with this finisher. Then there was 'not for nothing' from the head of the team. Of course, his was an idiom that means what's about to be said or done is not in vain; that it has a cause, a purpose, a reason or a use.

Mine was, yes, 'quick and dirty'. Though I should probably say 'is', as I still use it far too often. Honestly, I think it really gets to the core of what working with smart people in a collaborative way is all about: iterating, fast, and reviewing, together. 'Give me the quick and dirty version of those numbers, of that analysis, of the prep for the big meeting. First thoughts, fast. Then we can puzzle out how to improve it, together, even faster.'

My second most oft-used phrase, however, was a little more brutal and a little less suggestive: 'The first five years of work are always a bit shit.'

This one wasn't, isn't, in my day-to-day use. But it does come up remarkably frequently in those quiet heart-to-hearts when resolve is wavering and doubts are setting in. There is a second part which I normally add on too. Along these lines: 'Year two is less worse than year one. Year three is less worse than year two, and so on. But it doesn't start getting objectively good *at least* until year five and beyond.'

STAY ON THE BUS

My thesis on career paths worth following is that the start is *always* hard. It gets progressively less hard. But still, hard.

It's not just me. And it's not just investment banking.

The Finish-American photographer Arno Minkkinen illustrates these truths with a tale about Helsinki bus station, and how all the buses that leave it follow the same route at the start, before peeling off on their unique suburban paths.[1] He uses this as a metaphor for being an artist: that at the start, by definition, you are following the same route as many others, but that with time you will branch out and find your own road of creativity.

Speaking at a university graduation ceremony, he tells his audience that at some point early on they will be shocked to realise that in those first few years their work turns out to be a derivative of another, more famous, artist's. And upon this realisation, they might 'hop off the bus, grab a cab (because life is short) and head straight back to the bus station looking for another platform', another artistic direction, because surely the first one was the wrong one? But the same thing happens again, and potentially again.

Minkkinen implores these budding photographers to 'stay on the bus. Stay on the fucking bus. Why, because if you do, in time you will begin to see a difference.' Eventually, he tells his audience, and us, that the bus routes diverge, just like our own paths, or the paths of these photographers, who will, with time, find their own artistic voices and paths

Minkkinen's focus through this allegory is the very real challenge of pursuing a creative path. But the lessons that he teaches are universally applicable. And I am not the only one of this opinion. When you google 'Helsinki bus station theory' (and please do: read his entire speech – these snippets and my summary barely do it justice), you will find piece after piece connecting the lessons of, ahem, staying on the fucking bus, to teaching, becoming a counsellor, doing doctoral research, the path of entrepreneurship and much more.

The message here is for all of us. The dials framework can help with this because it captures some element of life taking time, of being dynamic and responsive, and not always fully in your control. You will have your dashboard values and priorities – maybe these are about being a renowned photographer. But the dials that express that, and the levels at which those dials are set – studying photography, shooting weddings and family portraits on the weekends while you hone your craft and keep a roof over your head, and getting to visit Helsinki on holiday one year – are ways to get comfortable with the inevitable time that all of this will take, and to enjoy the process along the way.

THE PSYCHOLOGICAL DISCOMFORT OF THE START

The start, by definition, is where psychological discomfort is exceptionally high. Psychological discomfort is a 'lasting, unsustainable, and unpleasant feeling resulting from negative appraisal of an inability or deficiency of the self. This negative self-appraisal is typically brought on by loss of someone or something, or failure to achieve something that is intimately linked to core psychological needs.'[2]

There is barely a word in that definition that doesn't *scream* about what the start of a meaningful career is. The cool jobs, the satisfying jobs, the ones that contribute to the three core psychological needs of autonomy, competence and relatedness are also, by definition, the ones where there is no singular perfect way of doing them.[3] They require creativity, the combining of hard and soft skills, and deft navigation of people, organisations and concepts. It is the inverse of Leo Tolstoy's famous opening line in *Anna Karenina*: 'Happy families are all alike; every unhappy family is unhappy in its own way'.[4] **There are countless ways of being successful in any given one of these psychologically satisfying roles. But all those who fail will fail for a very similar set of reasons.**

I look around the trading floor and I see numerous excellent salespeople but not one of them doing it in the exact same way as the next: some focus on razor-sharp quantitative knowledge of markets, others on the ability to build deep and trusted relationships over the long term, others on the skills of structuring the perfect trade format, others on being the person you want to call with the best stories about the weekend on a Monday morning. Yes, every person has the core set of skills that the job requires, but what makes them successful is that they have found their own, authentic way to do a role that has definable outputs but indefinable inputs.

The utter look of horror that descends upon the faces of those with whom I've shared my theory of 'The Progressively Less Shit Years' is grim to behold: 5 years to a 21- or 23-year-old is an impossibly long time. Hell, five months is an impossibly long period of time to anyone who is having severe doubts about the path they are on. Especially one they have chosen and often fought so hard to be on.

Yet, the message I so desperately want to convey with this saying is much more positive than it first appears.

Firstly, you are not alone. Many, many people at the start of careers – irrespective of age and stage – feel like this. The start being, well, a bit shit, doesn't mean life has to be shit. We will get deeply into this in the next chapter.

Secondly, it improves, rapidly. The Progressively Less Shit Years is not a catchy slogan, and nor does it capture the truth that these years won't feel like total shit when you are in them. But the contrast of the improvement year on year will feel so good that you will question this very concept. Until one day, you get to the intrinsically good stuff of being in a role and/or a place in your career where it all clicks. Where you are getting to do something that suits you and your skill set so well that the challenges feel empowering instead of crushing. And *then* you'll look back and see The Progressively Less Shit Years in your rear-view mirror. Not least because the transaction costs of quitting are themselves high: a large 12-wave study of over 4,000 job changers found on average that it took around five years for people to get back to their satisfaction levels from their past jobs. This was true even though people generally left due to dissatisfaction in the first place.[5]

> **Chris**
> *I think I am just out of these years. They are so obvious in hindsight, and so impossible to see at the time. Now I recognise my own value in terms of the skills I have, and the value those have in the world. I am more in control of what I can do and where. When you are starting out, you don't know the specifics of a role or a job, or the culture or how any of this stuff works. It takes years. Just being along for the ride has more value than you think.*

Thirdly, what is on the other side of the beginning is *so* worth having. The number one cause of career failure on many of the most fulfilling and rewarding paths isn't not working hard enough, or not being smart enough, or not being unique enough – it is quitting before the going gets good. **You need to stay to reap the biggest benefits: interesting content, roles that better suit your skills and preferences, control over your time, highest pay, operating in a state of 'flow'.** The first few years of almost all careers are decidedly *not* all those things. Many times, quitting is resetting the timer rather than escaping it.

A piece of what makes getting through the innate toughness of the beginning comes from the gentle but persistent background hum in society that we should all be Mark Zuckerberging our way through life: coming up with huge, new ideas and executing them at pace, all while terrifyingly young and terrifyingly without self-doubt. That if you are following an oft-travelled path, one that may not have quick or huge obvious success, that you lack creativity or are rejecting excitement for a life of trudging drudgery. Author Oliver Burkeman describes it as such: 'in many areas of life, there's strong cultural pressure to strike out in a unique direction' and not to follow the herd when it comes to marriage, work, children.[6]

No one wants to be, or even think of themselves as, unexciting and unoriginal. 'Yet,' Oliver argues, 'if you always pursue the unconventional in this way, you deny yourself the possibility of experiencing those other, richer forms of uniqueness that are reserved for those with the patience to travel the well-trodden path first.'

This is not some critique of snowflake Millennials (being one myself – a Millennial, that is; someone else will have to opine on the snowflake part). Nor is it a cry to lean in and work harder, sacrificing your body, mind and soul on the altar of 'success'. In fact, often the answer is slightly less at work and a lot more outside of it (again, more on this later in the book). But this is a push to staying through the start. Because **the start of careers worth having is almost *always* hard**.

That feeling of having no idea what the hell you are doing, of having no clue at all how you are meant to do the things which are being asked of you, is *because* you are on a path which will, eventually, allow you to fulfil your core psychological needs. The roles, the jobs, the careers that are full of autonomy and generate competence and that breed relatedness are the ones where it takes time to work out what works. For you, for your roles and for your career.

So many of us feel that desperation at the beginning. That sense of flailing. Even failing. The analysts at an investment bank. The newly qualified doctors. The fledgling entrepreneurs. Hell, even actors. Daisy Edgar-Jones who starred in the 2020 lockdown breakout smash hit *Normal People* describes that experience as such: 'I was very green as an actor. There were times I thought, my God, I don't know what I'm doing, I'm too wee. There was this thought that if I had one bad day at work I'd have to live with the results for the rest of my life.'[7]

I am not the C-Suiter or founder or gazillionaire, but I am in a good place in a great career not because I worked harder, or because I am smarter, or because I was better connected. I am here because of two things: luck, in that the stars aligned to get the opportunity in the first place, and because *I stayed.* I stayed long enough to get past the panic of unmet psychological needs and to discover what the roles required and how I could uniquely best do them. I could, and did, constantly check back to my dashboard that the choices I was making spoke to what my values, goals and priorities for my life were, and that I was expressing them, albeit in a nascent way, in my dials.

It wasn't, however, that I was always sure I wanted to stay the course. Or even that I thought I could. I had the same doubt and anxiety that is a feature of these types of paths.

The first wobble I had was right at the beginning. I'm not even sure I should call it a wobble as that would suggest I had reached a level of stability which then got disturbed. In fact, I found it bone-shatteringly shaky from the start. After long, scary days full of errors and self-doubt, I'd walk slowly back to my flat and call my parents in floods of tears, telling them the only thing I was sure of was that I'd made a massive mistake.

So much so that after a year I decided to revert to my teenage plan of going into the civil service, applying for a fast-stream position at Her Majesty's Treasury. Towards the end of the four months it took for a polite, but firm rejection to arrive (I was ranked a C+ in their assessment: too many strident opinions apparently!), I got a call from a headhunter about a role at a prestigious American investment bank. I interviewed and liked the people more than I ever expected to. Figuring that finishing my investment banking career with this firm on my CV would be no bad thing (because surely, I would have all the same issues doing the same job at a new place, and more fool them for wanting me), I accepted. Quitting, but not *quitting*. Quitting my employer, but not my career path. A new firm and some more time would give me a few more data points with which to work it out.

The first of those was not what I expected. It was a realisation that hatred of the feeling that I had no idea what I was doing would be both temporary *and* permanent.

Temporary because I was passing through The Progressively Less Shit Years. I was learning more and getting more right, or mostly just getting less wrong. The terror was subsiding, slightly. Things were starting to make sense, slowly, but surely. Soon I would be out of the worst. I probably already was, even if the objectively good stuff was a little further off.

Permanent because careers are about progression, which means repeatedly doing new things and being out of your comfort zone. This cycle would, by definition, repeat. Again and again and again. However, it would never be quite as hard as that first time. Because, forever onwards, I would have the lived experience of having been through it before. I would *know* that I could not only survive but thrive. That the experience of feeling profoundly out of my depth, finding my footing and then, eventually, mastery, would be so satisfying that I would want to do it more than once. That things felt hard because they *were* hard. But that was OK. I could do hard things. I even liked to do them. And therein lies the permanence.

Once I realised, and accepted, this simultaneously scary and somewhat freeing truth, it gave me some space to collect a second data point – this one more personal to me and my career, and my choices: that I really enjoyed working with really smart people, solving really complicated problems and getting paid really well for it. I liked being on a busy trading floor, full of life and personalities. I was good at navigating a big, complex organisation and getting stuff done within it. I loved the certainty of my income and the earning trajectory that lay ahead of me. And I realised that these were some of the defining features of what role I wanted career to play in my life. Day-to-day, year-to-year and #lifegoal wise. What was – is – on my dashboard.

Finding ways to express your dashboard values and priorities or to reach your goals as they evolve is going to require new dials and setting them at new levels, time and time again. My goals, of course, are not the things that might be important to you or, frankly, to anyone else, which is kind of the point. When we discussed back in Chapter 4 what is important, it is about the importance in *your* life. Thank goodness there are a bunch of you with 'helping people' or 'inventing things' or 'solving the climate crisis' on your dashboards. Or values like community or experimentation. There might be a topic that you are so deeply fascinated by that doing anything other than spending your days on it is sacrilege. Thank *goodness* for you! But that is not me. I like hopping from topic to topic, I like working with intense people in intense environments. And once I'd got some perspective, I could separate the challenges of the early years of an intellectually challenging career from the challenges of working out who I was, what I wanted and where I could thrive.

Next time you find yourself in the swirl of the challenge of separating out the natural difficulties of the start from inklings that a path or choice may not be the right one for you, take a moment to check back in with all three parts of your Dials framework.

Questions to ask yourself

- Does this choice or path get you closer to meeting a goal on your dashboard?
- Does it reflect the values or priorities on your dashboard?
- Does this feel so hard because you have all the other dials in your life turned down too low, or too high?
- Is it possible for you to turn those other dials back up, or down, or add dials that you are missing? Or is this choice or path preventing that?

_____

_____

_____

_____

This process is a really powerful one: checking back to see if your work, or indeed other components, other dials of life, are expressing the values, goals and priorities you laid out in your dashboard. If they are, then maybe the challenge you are facing is 'just' the natural texture of the path you are walking. If not, perhaps it speaks to a more fundamental misalignment that needs addressing.

Rowan

It feels like such a cliché to say I am now a digital nomad. It's not that I didn't enjoy what I was doing before. It was a really high-status job and career path: I was working in the NHS. Everyone was so proud of me for doing it, and I was proud of it too. I was helping people and it mattered, especially during the COVID-19 pandemic. But I really struggled with how contained my life was and how any impact I was having was very one-on-one. Now I am travelling and

*working wherever I want. I am brimming with ideas and so
full of excitement bringing them to life, creating. And helping people in a different, much broader way.*

*Don't get me wrong, I miss working in a team and even
having a 'place of work', but it is so clear to me now that
my work and my values are aligned. I was meant to do this,
I am meant to be here. I don't feel like I've quit. I've just
found a much better way of doing my purpose.*

WHEN QUITTING IS THE BEST OPTION

I am not saying to *never* quit, but to stay long enough to make
the decision to stay or go based not on fear, or doubt, or lack
of knowledge about your skills and values, but on a fundamental knowledge about yourself and what you want to and
can do.

Maybe I am wrong about those lessons taking exactly five
years to learn. Maybe it is two or three, or seven. This is meant
to be an imprecise, but helpful, rule of thumb that speaks to the
fact that these lessons do take time. They do require, sometimes,
staying on the, ahem, fucking bus.

So, when is the time for quitting?

**Quitting is essential if you find yourself in a situation that
is detrimental to your mental or physical health.** This is non-
negotiable. Nothing is worth risking the things that truly matter
– the very things we discussed back in Chapter 5, that help you
stay resilient. Dials like your health, or rest, or time in nature. If
you are burning out, not sleeping, not being respected, not being
heard when you raise issues, feeling dread or have stopped
caring about your performance, then these are all classic signs
that your mental health is at risk. And quitting not only should
be an option but may well be the only right and urgent choice. I
cannot emphasise this enough.

There is a gulf of difference, however, between this and the very real but very different challenges of being out of your comfort zone and discovering your unique path through life – stumbles and challenges and all. A call to 'not quit' must never give anyone around you a green light to treat you badly. Quite the opposite: colleagues, managers, mentors, sponsors, firms should be going out of their way to give extra support and to strip out things in your work that are challenging but without any purpose or pay-off. This is precisely why the culture of 'I did it when I was starting out therefore nothing needs to change' is so damaging.

Dr Susan David is an award-winning Harvard Medical School psychologist and specialist in all things management. In her book *Emotional Agility* one of the questions she tackles is this: the one of 'when to grit vs. when to quit'.[8] Of course, she can no more answer it for you and your individual circumstance than I can, yet the questions she poses do hone in on the essence of the issues at hand here. David asks us to ask ourselves if we find what we are doing brings us joy or satisfaction, and if deep down we believe that we can be successful. Does what you are doing reflect your values in life and are you playing to your strengths? And finally, she urges us to consider what we are giving up in order to keep doing what we are doing.

Notice that whether you are having a good time at every exact moment is not one of David's questions. Learning new things is hard. Being out of your comfort zone is hard. Being in psychological discomfort as you create a life where your psychological needs are fully met, in this world that we all currently exist in, is hard. However, the perseverance to stay, all that effort and determination to keep going, must be in service of your values and your goals (your dashboard) and how you like to live your day to day (your dials).

This is precisely how quitting can be the thing that you need to do, but not in a way that is about escaping the negative. Rather, it's about pivoting to the positive. It's about moving on to something better. Author and journalist Elizabeth Day describes it as 'the pleasure of giving up', saying that now she is in a position in her life and career when she can 'quit for positive reasons – not because anything is wrong but because many things are right and I want to see what happens when I say yes to new opportunities'.[9] Day shared this vignette while writing about the decision to end her weekly magazine column. She remains a bestselling fiction and non-fiction author, and award-winning podcaster and broadcaster.

It is so easy to look at people like this who seemingly have it all sorted and think it is easy for them. *Of course* the bestselling author and podcaster can quit positively. But that is the point: for nearly all of us, the good stuff *takes time.* Careers snowball. Skills build. Knowledge deepens. Networks expand. Safety nets solidify. Failures transform. Mistakes correct. Doubts fade.

Give yourself some time to do the work.

MAKING IT POSSIBLE TO STAY

If the decision is to stay, then there is one more essential consideration, making that experience of the diminishing, but very real, toughness of those early years more manageable. Because this isn't about toughing it out regardless or, ugh, 'sucking it up'. The way to stay, the way to give yourself the maximum opportunity to learn about yourself and the options around you is *to not be miserable.* And the way to do that is to have all the other things that make life worth living – a multifaceted, deep, interesting and varied life, not just one homogenous lump of this that is 'not work'.

And *this* is where the rest of your dials come in. This is where it matters that you have all the other component parts of life that make your days joyful. Or that mean you get a sense of achievement from somewhere which is not the office. Or that you have people in your life who you can support or praise or just be silly with who have absolutely nothing to do with your work.

Chapter 7

LIVING A RICH AND VARIED LIFE

I KNEW I had rebroken the bone the moment I hit the concrete. But denial is a powerful emotion. And I was in it.

It was a Sunday evening in March 2016. Less than a month after I turned 30. Less than 21 months after I broke my collarbone for the first time getting hit by a van while cycling to work. Less than 18 months after I had started yoga to help heal the soft tissue damage to my shoulder that went with the break.

And I'd done it again. Broken a collarbone that is, falling out of a handstand that I had no business trying, into a crumpled heap on my concrete kitchen floor. Well, not 'a' collarbone. *The* collarbone. The same one attached to my dominant right arm. The same one which I all too deeply knew would make it impossible to sleep, or get dressed independently, or laugh, or not be terrified of someone bumping into me in the street for several weeks.

I walked, very quietly and very gingerly, into the living room and sat next to my husband on the sofa. In total denial. For about 17 minutes.

Because that was how long it took for the physical reaction in my body – the shock, the pain and the horror of the knowledge that I'd have to spend the next few weeks wandering around with an unset broken bone at the core of my body – to overwhelm my absolutely ignoring reality brain.

I turned to my left and said to my husband Nick: 'I've broken my collarbone again.'

It took a beat for him to process what he was hearing. And even then, he blinked at me, confused: 'Er, but you've just been sitting there?!'

Cue 30 minutes of silent sobbing and attempts to calm down, which eventually involved cutting me out of my sports bra with a pair of kitchen shears, followed by a trip to A&E the next morning to confirm the inevitable.

As this is the start of my 'have a hobby' pitch, I've probably got off on the wrong foot. Do yoga! Break bones! Ruin your Sunday night! But honestly, breaking my collarbone was one (or should I say two?) of the most formative experiences of my non-work non-relationship adult life.

The first time, it led me to take up yoga – something that has transformed my mental and physical health and resilience. The second time, it taught me humility and a depth of understanding about myself and the strengths and weaknesses of my personality that I needed to get a handle on once and for all. And became something I knew would be a part of my life, for life.

It's still shocking and frankly embarrassing to say that it was a collarbone break rather than the near-death experience and heart/lung damage that was pulmonary embolisms (PEs – see page 64) which taught me this latter lesson, but it was. The first time with the PEs, I felt 'lucky'. Not that it had happened, but that I hadn't died, of course, and that the treatment was straightforward, and I ultimately made a full recovery. It has changed the course of my experience of pregnancy and birth (both of which are now high-risk events for me), but, that aside, I do and should be able to continue living a normal life.

The second collarbone break, however, was all on me. The first time I could blame it on the van driver, but this one was absolutely *my fault*. There was no way I was ready to be messing around with handstands that early in my yoga practice. I was way out of my depth physically and I knew it. But I ignored those thoughts and the physical signals, just as I had the early warning signs of the PEs (the breathlessness, the weight loss), even though they had been much more severe. The second bone break was a massive wake-up call that I had to start prioritising my physical health in a way I never had before. I had to start *listening*.

In short, everyone deserves a yoga accident. And I'm only half joking.

I don't wish a broken bone or other calamity on anyone. (Please let me not do it a third time.) But what I do wish for everyone is the chance to have more brutally honest, totally sideways and different life experiences. **To invite serendipity in – by design. To give randomness a chance – by choice. To learn more, live better and hopefully fall in love with something that is *not* work.** To find something that is fun enough that you want to be doing it on a Sunday night. And return to it even when you fuck it up. And maybe even when you hurt yourself. To have something, even many things, that you get to do because they explore and reveal other parts of your personality. They scratch itches you didn't know you had and help you discover and solidify who you are and what makes you tick.

Things that you do not have to monetise. Babies, and hobbies, and adventures, and books. Boyfriends, girlfriends, lovers, one-night stands. Art, culture, family, friends, volunteering. Naps.

Music. Fashion. Theatre. Pottery. Long walks. Longer afternoons slobbing on the sofa and completing Netflix series. Cousins, nieces, nephews, sports teams, dance moves, guitar solos. Gardening. Festivals. Travels, holidays, city breaks. And anything and everything in between. These are so many of the things that I hope are already earmarked on your dials. And let's be very clear: each and every one of them is worth its weight in gold in and of itself. Full stop.

Yet, I don't think anyone needs me to persuade them *why* having all the pieces of a broad and bold and colourful life is both great and totally necessary. What so many of us struggle with is giving ourselves permission to live like this – to make the space in our lives for this truth to shine through. Because, well, work. And responsibilities. And deadlines. And bills. And and and . . .

'A life', however, is an *essential* part of any successful career. Let me say that another way: you will find it infinitely harder to reach your full potential in your work and in your career if you do not build yourself a series of things you love into your existence that are not about your job or money.

A life is a *feature* of what makes a career successful, not a bug.

So express it in your dials. Not one reductive 'life' bucket, but several, even many, dials. Dials which individually and together represent all the non-work components of life that bring fun, and joy, and adventure, and love, and more. By having them there, by thinking about them explicitly in this way, you will have a constant reminder not to let this essential truth slip you by.

Questions to ask yourself

- What is in your life which brings you joy?
- What are the things that you do, or indeed would like to do outside of work?
- If you were responsibility-free for a day or a week, how would you spend your time?
- Is there anything here that you haven't already sketched out as a dial? Remember, it might not be able to be turned up to the max right now, but you cannot turn up a dial, a part of your life, which you haven't started to give space to.

_____

_____

_____

_____

Have these dials on your dashboard. Give them space in your life. Allow them to be wonderful component parts of your life themselves, _and_ to help your career and your work be all it needs to be for you.

Nadia

What brings me joy is quality time with my favourite people doing something active and exciting: skiing, hiking, surfing, wild swimming. I want to learn to kite surf. It's been on my list forever. This is a new dial I'd like to put on dashboard. Even if I'm not going to be able to turn it up until I can manage a trip to Morocco to learn.

CREATING ENERGY FOR YOUR WORK

A rich and varied life is not an add-on when things finally calm down enough to do that class or see that friend or take that trip.

It is not something that gets in the way of you working hard or doing your best in your role. It is, instead, an utterly fundamental component of your job performance and the success of your career.

'A life' can very much feel like *a bad idea* at any time in some careers. People might even tell you it's a bad idea at multiple points. But it *must* be expressed in your dials. And you *must* turn up the levels on the component parts more often than you think. **Because the reality is that having a bunch of these things alongside your work makes your career *better*.**

All these things breed energy. And nothing, *nothing* consumes more of that than careers. They can be so full of doubt, and risk, and difficulty. They feel hard, because they are hard. Yes, careers are also full of all the good stuff like achievement and learning and, let's be honest, money. But it's rarely a straightforward, hazard-free path. Even on the best of days – the kick-ass presentations, the moments of creative flair, the times you close the deal – the amount of yourself you must commit, to show up with, to *give*, is vast. This is even truer if you are doing this in places where there are not a lot of people who look like you or who come from where you have.

Much of the energy you will expend comes from your inner reserves: your life goals, your mission, your purpose and your values – all the things which are reflected in your dashboard. And while your dashboard is utterly necessary, it is still insufficient on this front. You also need things which are going to fill up your energy reserves. Regularly. Even daily. People to inspire you. Events to excite you. Achievements, small and large, which remind you that you can do hard things. That you can learn, and try and fail, and try again and be all the better for it. There is a real virtuous circle that occurs here. **When you have the additional fuel from all the other components in your life, you**

have more energy and fire for work. The positivity and self-belief accumulate upwards in a wonderfully exponential way.

For me, is not that the act of yoga itself – lengthening my hamstrings or balancing on my forearms or pretzeling my back – has made me specifically any better at convening senior people or disentangling tricky business situations. But when I can show up having spent a bunch of time doing things I love, I can handle those challenges to the best of my ability. **Having a reservoir of recent lived experience of being a version of yourself that you are confident in, shines through to the situations where you might be less confident.** Even if, sometimes, the contrast between the two can take your breath away.

Your time is not a zero-sum game. On this front at least. One hour spent taking a walk along the river, chatting to an old friend, making bread, learning a new martial art or curling up on the sofa with a book is not mathematically an hour you could have been at your desk producing your Very Best Work. Not only does productivity nosedive beyond a certain point (a Stanford professor found that productivity per hour worked declines sharply beyond 50 hours a week and that those working up to 70 hours a week are only getting as much done as those working 55)[1] but your Very Best Work *requires* you to have energy and ideas and a willingness to take risks. Philosopher Alexander den Heijer describes it this way: 'You often feel tired, not because you've done too much, but because you've done too little of what sparks light in you.'[2]

The way this discussion often plays out in the real world hops from this point to the assertion that it is the work itself which should be sparking light. And if it doesn't, you are doing the wrong work or the work wrong.

This is a legacy of the old ways of working: that you must be 'all-in' in your career. That it must be your passion and your mission. And by logical extension, if you are spending any meaningful amount of time doing other things, you are demonstrably not taking it seriously enough. That you are not committed enough. This, after all, was the genesis of 'face time': bosses wanted (want?) to *see* that you were choosing your work above all other options. The next chapter takes a deeper look at the perils of the 'make your passion your work and you'll never work a day in your life' approach. For now, however, the point is that you can, do and should find things that spark joy beyond your work.

Questions to ask yourself
- When was the last time you achieved something that wasn't in your work or school life?
- When was the last time you strived for something that wasn't about output or income?
- When was the last time you gave yourself some space to take a risk or try something new that didn't have your reputation or future depending on it?

_____

_____

_____

_____

HOW SKILLS CAN COMBINE

There are vanishingly few careers where broader experiences won't make you better at them. US Supreme Court Justice and feminist pioneer, Ruth Bader Ginsburg articulated it as such: 'My success in law school, I have no doubt, was in large measure because of baby Jane. I attended classes and studied diligently until four in the afternoon and then it was "Jane's time", which she spent relaxing, having fun, doing whatever she wanted until bedtime. After that, she would return to studying. 'Each part of my life provided respite from the other and gave me a sense of proportion that classmates trained only on law studies lacked.'[3] When skills and experiences from surprising places come together, wonderful new things can happen.

Another famous example of this is Steve Jobs' calligraphy story – one which Jobs told at a commencement address he gave at a university in 2005. He spoke about dropping out of college but still dropping into classes that took his fancy. One of which was a calligraphy class which was of no use to him at the time – nor could he foresee how it would become useful to him – until he remembered what he had learnt in that class 10 years later when he was creating the first Macintosh computer. 'It was the first computer with beautiful typography,' Jobs said in his speech. 'If I had never dropped in on that single course in college, the Mac would have never had multiple typefaces or proportionally spaced fonts.'[4]

We are all more than the simple sum of our parts. Those parts smoosh together and interact in a myriad of unexpected ways. Creating something new, something unexpected. Something *more*.

But the quantity and quality of the parts that we put into that chemistry experiment still matter: 99 per cent work and 1 per cent anything else is not going to make an exciting or interesting mix.

RELEASING THE CAREER DEATH GRIP
People quit great career paths not because they don't want to work hard or that they aren't smart or creative. They quit because they are miserable. And the one way – directly in your control – to not be miserable is to have a range of other dials on

your dashboard, as well as the work ones, which make life worth living. Not at the 'end' once you have time and money and mental space to throw at it all. But now. Along the way. Today. This year. Now.

There is a 'stick-with-it-ness' that careers require. A riding the rough with the smooth, learning and improving skills, building a network, looking for and seizing opportunities when they come, honing a craft – all things that take time. Having a bunch of 'other' parts of life – such as meaningful relationships and experiences and chances to find mastery and purpose and autonomy beyond your work – will enable you to give your career the time it needs to blossom. They make your career more resilient.

This isn't about being patient or waiting for your turn or putting up with being treated badly. Anyone who knows me or has had the misfortune of managing me will know I am *hugely* career impatient, still. I am very much guilty of barely taking a moment to celebrate the win or the milestone before searching for the next step and asking for more, even if I'm not quite ready (again, sorry to all my bosses who must gently – or not so gently – point out what I need to improve on first).

This is about taking a cold hard look at what is in your locus of control and managing *that*. Because, straight up, your career timeline is rarely one of those things. No matter how hard you work or how smart you are or how hard you hustle, you cannot simply *decide* that now is the time for a promotion or a new job or to raise the funding for your start-up, or that you have the perfect melody for that song you must write. You can take all the steps to make those things more likely to happen, but some of it is just out there in the hands of others, at best, or a bunch of randomness, at worst, to decide.

We live in a world where you cannot perfectly control your

career path or timing. So, it pays to make that dance with time bearable. Or, even better, enjoyable. It is about being able to stay the course. Not through sheer grit and determination, but because there are other things you can and do turn to which fill you up. Other things which give you a sense of forward motion and achievement and identity.

This identity point is not a small one. A flippant piece of advice on this front is not to let work become your life. This can happen in the obvious way of spending all the hours of all the days working, to the extent that you simply have no time for anything non-work. But there is a deeper way in which this can be true – that work becomes your sole identity. When you only have one big thing through which you express to yourself and the world who you are, what you are capable of and what you value, that one thing suddenly becomes terrifyingly precious. And you start holding on to it terrifyingly tightly. A death grip which kills the very thing you are so protective of.

When work is your life it means it is your primary identity. Making a mistake doesn't just become an opportunity to learn or a natural part of the process of being human and improving your work. It becomes a near-death experience. One where everything you care about and have worked so hard for is suddenly at risk.

Getting stuck working alongside an arsehole on a new project stops being an annoyance, albeit a serious one, that you can shake off once you leave the building. It comes home with you. It affects how you interact with the people you love. Or you double down on an error in a spreadsheet or a missed email on an important assignment and cover up instead of owning up, making a forgettable instance snowball into a question mark about your integrity.

When work is the only thing you feel like you are making progress on, and that progress falters, the sense of worthlessness and doubt this engenders can be paralysing – the missed promotion, the failed pitch, the not-got new job all become so self-defining that it is easier to self-destruct.

The risks of burnout

The hardest thing to square about all of this is that it threatens the very thing you have prioritised, that you are trying to foster: your career. You grasp on to it so fiercely that it cannot withstand the pressure. It is in this direction that burnout and other horrors lie.

Because no matter how hard you work or how talented you are, the work odds aren't going to roll in your favour every single time. Over a lifetime, the iterations should. Not least because you will have found a broad and flexible enough way to define your goals, values and priorities that they – and your happiness – do not hang on binary 'successes' or 'failures'. Success, achievement, sense of self and purpose all can and should be found in work *and* in the rest of your life. You having a life – a broad and deep and colourful one – is valuable to any work and career which is lucky enough to have you.

The good news is that this is becoming more well-known and properly evidenced. Life satisfaction has been proven to be associated with higher career satisfaction, organisational commitment and job satisfaction, as well as productivity.[5]

Employers are increasingly recognising the importance of this too: 88 per cent of companies in the US are investing more in mental health, more than 80 per cent are spending more on stress-management and resilience resources, and more than half of the companies surveyed were offering new mindfulness and meditation programmes.[6] All to combat crises such as employee burnout, something that has become so severe that the World Health Organization (WHO) has now officially recognised burnout as an occupational phenomenon – the first step on a path to them developing evidence-based guidelines on mental well-being in the workplace.[7]

There is, of course, some enlightened self-interest in companies acting on this front. The cost of replacing an employee is typically one-and-a-half to two times that person's salary. Research shows that a 100-person organisation that provides an average salary of $50,000 could have turnover and replacement costs of approximately $660,000 to $2.6 million *per year*.[8] At pre-pandemic turnover rates, that translates to nearly $1 trillion a year for US businesses alone, which is obviously huge, but may still be too low an assessment. Further research takes these numbers and shows they fail to consider the very real network effect of departures, meaning the impact of the leaver's departure on their co-workers' productivity.[9] On average, most employees are relied upon by 5 to 12 colleagues, so a conservative estimate at the lower end of that range and assuming a small, but significant, hit to productivity of 5 per cent for 6 months, adds another $845,000 cost per leaver for inefficiencies in the network.

People need to be happy to do their best work. Firms need employees to be happy to get the best out of them. The mutual benefits are significant.

> **Questions to ask yourself**
> - Do you have all the component parts that allow you to be your best, be it rest, or relationships, or underwater basket-weaving?
> - What activity or which people or place leaves you feeling energised?
>
> _____
>
> _____
>
> _____

DOING THE (NON)WORK

No matter how accurate this data is and how increasingly well acknowledged it is in the world of work, there are still real hurdles on the path to building a life as well as a career. Because even if you work for an amazing firm, a wonderful boss or have built your own freelance portfolio or business, **we each still have to give ourselves the psychic permission to have a life.** Which is no small feat. For women in particular.

Philosopher Kate Manne describes the root cause of the challenge here as the societal convention that certain people, particularly women, are expected to be infinitely selfless, defined by their capacity to be 'human givers' rather than human *beings*.[10] This incisive observation really gets to the heart of the supposed conflict between motherhood and work: for a perfect mother is one who is giving all she can to her children, the perfect wife all to her husband, while a perfect worker is giving all to their job. Surely anyone doing the latter cannot do the former at the same time. Forget about all the other pieces of a life we are talking about here. And, of course, fathers are just as hurt by the flip side of this trap: all work, no caring.

The guilt, the fear of not giving any of these things your all can feel almost inescapable when these are the expectations which have been seeping into us over decades and decades. Even when all the logic and all the research shows that the very opposite is true. Having these non-work components of life as individual dials is one way to help you give yourself this permission.

It took living some of this out to finally give myself the permission to believe and permanently commit to running my life this way. It began when I hit a milestone a few years ago, which should have been less painful than a concrete floor – in theory. That milestone was 10,000 followers on Instagram.

In a world full of influencers, one which is saturated by social media platforms and where every man, his dog and his business has profiles on all of them, this doesn't feel like a particularly big deal. However, back in 2016, none of those things were true. Especially for junior investment bankers with a love for yoga.

I had been somewhat secretive about both my ever-growing yoga habit and the social media platform that was enabling it up to this point. I didn't share my name on my Instagram (going by the moniker 'Somewhat RAD' – a play on my initials and the fact I very much knew that nothing about me was radical) or even the industry I worked in – hinting obliquely at a 'big career' and a busy life. This was pre-algorithm days, so it was a slow but steady climb once you somehow got some momentum, which for me stemmed back to cute cats and eye-catching before-and-after comparison photos as my body creaked towards some level of flexibility and strength. As the numbers creeped up, it dawned on me that I might need to tell 'The Firm', which at this point in time, still touching distance of the Great Financial Crisis of 2008, was understandably cautious regarding anything public-facing. Forget about this whole new and free-form world of social media. So, I told Compliance. And the news quickly filtered back to senior management.

There was no big bang of disapproval or command from on high, but it was clear it was causing some ripples. Maybe even some waves. And I panicked, my mind immediately going to the worst-case scenario: was it really worth throwing away a career for some pretty pictures on the internet?

So, I sought counsel. Some friendly faces, both at work and in my personal life, suggested that I might want to 'take it down'. I call them friendly faces because I know that these people had my very best interests, from their vantage points, at heart. And this was all pretty left field, with no obvious purpose. Right?

What most people glancing in didn't – couldn't – see, however, was how much yoga and, separately, Instagram (they are very much two different things) were making my career possible. The physical and spiritual practice of yoga was healing my body and calming my mind, enabling me to show up and use my full faculties to tackle the tricky situations and problems that I was paid to address. Instagram was a wonderful commitment device to keep me practising, and the growing sense of community I found there along with the little endorphin hits of growing my account and 'being good' at something outside my work life was becoming a positive force in my life.

The trading floor can be a high-stress environment, and I was for sure in a place where I was feeling that stress and holding on too tightly to my career as a result. It was the only thing that was giving me positive feedback about what I could achieve, and so when I misstepped – forgot to loop in the right senior person to a client escalation or pissed off the head of trading at a huge client – it felt so calamitous that I was often paralysed by fear. I couldn't see that these things are par for the course and that I could steer myself and the situation back on to a good track. I hid, which is the very worst thing you can do when things are going wrong: that is precisely when you need enough confidence in your overall abilities and your understanding of the situation to reach out to the right people, explain what is going on and together find a way to fix it.

Yoga and Instagram together were bringing so much to my life away from work. Which, in and of themselves, was enough to not want to stop. But more than that, now I had really been forced to examine whether I was going to compromise – both being inextricably linked for me at this point, I knew how they were helping me with my career and it wasn't a realistic option for me to 'take it down'.

And therein lies an important nugget of truth that is applicable beyond me or yoga or investment banking. **The counterfactual isn't always an available option. There is often the way you are doing it, or no way at all.**

I am convinced that I would have blown up in some spectacular way if I hadn't had yoga grounding me, healing me; if I hadn't had Instagram giving me a creative outlet and helping me forge an identity beyond my work. Sure, it might have been nice to imagine it was possible for me to do my career the way others were – all late nights and football games and endless confidence and that. But looking honestly at myself, my situation, my strengths and my weaknesses, this was the only conclusion I could – can – draw.

This is what the easy-to-say but hard-to-understand description of doing life or a career in an authentic way really boils down to: that you do it the only way that is possible for you, even when that, at first, looks strange or scary to other people.

And it is why generic mental models like work–life balance are so damaging. Each of us has to find our own ways of doing this thing called life. We cannot be striving for someone else's version. We have to find our own. *You* have to find your own. And I hope The Dials can be the scaffolding that enables you to quickly, and easily, build that for yourself.

I politely demurred the few times I was gingerly questioned about whether it was a good idea to continue with my yoga account, when there were gentle suggestions that it was just too distracting and that it was all taking away from conversations that would have otherwise been about the quality of my work output and my commercial impact, or when tendrils of disapproval made their way through to me on the work gossip grapevine.

Instead, I drew some new boundaries about how and what I would share online and ultimately did the hardest thing of all – I gave myself permission to do my life and my work this way. My way.

Scroll forward a few years, and you can follow the very same firm on the very same platforms that once raised eyebrows. I made Managing Director a couple of years after that 10k milestone, when my follower count stood at over 100k, and just months after returning from my first maternity leave. It's hard not to think it worked out all right in the end.

The beauty of all this, of course, is that I will never know whether I would have blown up in the way I suspected. Or if my career would have taken off into the stratosphere if I hadn't thrown the slightly unusual spanner of social media into the trading floor works. But I sit here several years later and know, yes *know*, that **the only way of doing hard but worthwhile career things over prolonged periods of time is to do them in** a **sustainable and authentic way**. With a lot of other joy and fulfilment and living alongside.

HOW TO TURN YOUR WORK DIAL DOWN (A TOUCH)

By now, I hope I have convinced you of the essential nature of this 'having a life' business if you want a successful, long and enjoyable career. Which brings us to the million-dollar question: how the hell do you actually do it? Like really, really make it work in your life? Because so many of us still struggle with the practical steps.

Earlier in this chapter we discussed the frustrating reality that timelines and pace are one of the central uncontrollable realities of careers. They all have periods when they are racing ahead at stunning speed, and others caught in glass-smooth doldrums, fearfully doubting that any puff will fill the sails again. We've all had these lull moments. And we will again.

Putting this in the Dials framework, your career or work dial(s) will often dial *themselves* up and down. Instead of this solely being a cause of frustration, recast it as an opportunity. Use the time that comes along when your work dial isn't turned up to the max – when there isn't a promotion ahead or a big sexy project, or the perfect client, or or or . . .

Use the lulls to build a life. *This* is one of the many ways in which The Dials can be a framework that works practically for you.

> ### Joe
> *It's such a small thing, but I started reading books again when I restarted commuting three days a week after the COVID-19 lockdowns. The train journey is the perfect slot of time for it. I used to do work emails, but I'm happy with*

138

where I am in my career. I don't need to put the extra time in right now.

Time with my partner also brings me so much joy – the challenge is that, because, in theory, it can happen at any time, the risk and reality is that sometimes it happens for too little time. It's not like I have that obvious section of every day for it, like reading. Though thinking about it as a separate dial and where that is set to – currently too low – does make me want to address it.

These career lulls happen. Your work dial *will* get turned down at various junctures, whether you want it to or not. When it happens, and you have the financial breathing room to pause with it, seize a piece of that moment. Sign up for that Italian class. Cook a new recipe. Use the holiday days you keep rolling from year to year to year. Use the dialling up and dialling down to your advantage to build on all the other things that make a wonderful life. It matters in and of itself, and will help your career too.

Secondly, **know you can do all of this without grand gestures of commitment or formal flexibility or official approval**. All it took for for me when I started yoga classes was a couple of hours a week. I didn't need an official flexible working arrangement or a reduced working week. I didn't need official agreement from my boss: I was transparent about what I was doing and kept delivering the high quality of work needed because I was so full of energy and excitement about this new thing in my life.

It is amazing what you can get done in the seams of time you have available. Truly. And if you need more time or approval or whatever later on, then cross that bridge when you come to it.

A very real challenge for us all seeking inspiration on this front is that many of the people who have this cracked, across career types and locations and levels of seniority, still do it relatively on the down-low. It surprised me as much as anyone to find that full-time working corporate life, forget about trading floor life, would allow me the possibility to do so much yoga, to take a teacher-training course and teach, and to write books, until I lived it and discovered that there were many ingredients needed in the mix that in fact came much more readily *because* of corporate and trading floor life: steady and high income, generous holiday time and maternity benefits, and a fearlessness bred from knowing that yoga and books would never have to show up and put a roof over my family's head. Yet, no doubt informed by the zeitgeist conversations around investment banking and work–life balance, I had no idea until I stumbled into it.

There are so many people harbouring much more diverse lives than those that historically would have shown up on their (inevitably) illustrious business cards and LinkedIn pages. The helicopter pilot who is also a spinning teacher. The cardiologist who also writes novels. The estate agent who is also a tennis umpire. The physicist who is also a dancer. The army officer who is also a commissioned painter. The politician who is also a poet. The high-school maths teacher who wins mountain-biking competitions. The lobbyist who is a cordon bleu chef. The news presenter who moonlights as a child counsellor, or the TV producer who also teaches skiing.

This is Kate Manne's human giver versus human being conundrum again (see page 133). We *feel* our all is expected of us to excel at work. So, when we find some of that 'all' directed elsewhere, we are tempted to hide it because it feels like we are cheating. In fact, the reverse is often true. We are more likely to be able to give our best when we are enriched and enlivened and inspired by a whole lot of the other 'all' in our lives.

I only found out very recently that the saying 'a jack of all trades is a master of none' is not the entire phrase. The second half goes like this: 'but oftentimes better than a master of one'.

Questions to ask yourself

- What would 'permission' look like for you to have space for more 'non-work'? Who would you want to say yes to you, or which barrier would have to fall in order for it to be easier for you to action?

- Is it true that this barrier is immovable or that this person will say no, or that the only path forward includes them explicitly saying yes?

- What parcels of time in your week or month are currently underutilised or dead space that could be repurposed – 30 minutes here, an hour there? What would giving yourself permission and support to use this time in a new way look like for you?

_____

_____

_____

_____

Alex

I was pregnant during the COVID-19 pandemic and, with the lockdowns and working from home, I lived in my husband's cast-offs for the last few months of my pregnancy. It took that for me to realise that my wardrobe and what I wear matters to me. It took me living this period to realise that I felt like shit because I looked like shit. Wearing nice outfits makes me feel great. I enjoy the process of curating my wardrobe and shopping for the right new addition and talking to my friends about a new brand or something someone rented or found preloved.

It's so different to my day-to-day work, which is highly technical or now running around with a messy toddler at the weekends. It was a mix of recognising what I want and giving myself permission to spend more time – and a bit more money! – on it. It feels frivolous. Even saying it out loud. But it's not. Not to me.

Chapter 8

FINDING CAREER FULFILMENT

IT'S NOT QUITE as easy as 'one, two, three' (it never is, is it?), but there are three truths I want to illuminate here which further help us make sure that the work- and career-related dials on our dashboards are the right ones for us and that we create boundaries between them and our other dials. Ones that can help us find fulfilment in our careers.

DEVELOPING YOUR PASSIONS AND INTERESTS
When you've been married or in a relationship for a long time, you get to know your partner's stories really well. You know, their little go-to vignettes. The tales they share to illustrate a point.

A favourite of mine which my husband uses is one which starts with the doorbell ringing and ends with him telling a stranger that he isn't 14, but he is an agnostic Jew. He uses this one for a few different purposes: it can work for those 'having a bad day' stories, or looking a different age, or anything to do with religion. The caller was a Jehovah's Witness and made the sweet, if slightly bizarre, assumption that my bearded 30-something-year-old husband was the child of the household and asked whether his parents were in.

Whenever he tells this story I can't help feeling a tiny and still surprising pang of jealousy towards that Jehovah's Witness. I am not jealous of the formal religion, but the level of passion is quite remarkable. What a thing it is to have such a deep belief in something as intangible, to me at least, as a God that it drives you to spend large portions of your life knocking on random doors.

Religiosity has been in decline across the West over the past several decades: membership of the Church of England dropped from just over 40 per cent of the UK population in 1983 to under 17 per cent by 2014, while the proportion of the US population who are members of a church, mosque or synagogue dropped from 70 to 47 per cent from 1999 to 2018.[1,2] Over these same decades though, a different kind of fervour has been gaining strength: the deification to all things work. Writer Derek Thompson coined the term 'workism' in 2019 to describe this phenomenon.[3] He defines it as 'the belief that work is not only necessary to economic production, but also the centrepiece of one's identity and life's purpose', describing how work has transformed 'into a kind of religion, promising identity, transcendence and community'. Sound familiar?

We have all watched, and maybe even lived, this happening: the glorification of hustle culture, the celebration of the grind. Just this morning I pressed play on my podcast app and what was piped into my ears was a conversation between a founder of a billion-dollar company and the founder of a multi-million-dollar company about finding purpose 'beyond the 9 to 5'. He asked her whether she thought everyone had one, and she answered yes, going on to describe how to find your passion in life and turn that into your work, as each shared tales of working themselves to the point of having no contact with friends or family for prolonged periods of time. (Extra points awarded to those who didn't automatically assume the man founded the more valuable company!)

'Find your passion', 'Do what you love' and/or 'Love what you do' are the core, inescapable, tenets of this philosophy. Yet they push a falsehood about how passions actually work and, worse, one which sets many of us along paths which take us further away from the very things we are seeking. Getting back on track requires understanding an important truth: **passions aren't 'found', they are *developed*.**

Psychologists Carol Dweck and Gregory Walton, and social scientist Paul O'Keefe conducted a series of fascinating studies into this hypothesis.[4] They tested two approaches to interests on college students, a group of people who are so often advised to 'find' their passion and express it via their careers:

1. 'Fixed theory of interests': the idea that core interests are there from birth, just waiting to be discovered.
2. 'Growth theory': the idea that interests are something anyone can cultivate over time.

Their research found that fixed and growth theories of interest lead people to approach this essential component of life in quite different ways. A fixed theory reduced interest outside people's pre-existing interests: meaning they discount new information or experiences if they don't fit into topics they believe they are inherently passionate about. Which feels like a bad enough starting point in a world as full and diverse as ours, but there is more.

A fixed approach to passions leads people to anticipate that the passion itself will provide limitless motivation and, as such, pursuing it will not be difficult. When that expectation fails to materialise, because, well, #lifehappens, a fixed theory leads to 'a sharper decline in interest' than those with a growth approach. Meaning that people take the very existence of that difficulty as evidence that they weren't passionate about the thing in the first place. So they are cued to keep searching for their 'real passion', until a new (and totally natural) difficultly arises and proves to them again that they are on the wrong track. And they start again. Or judge themselves lacking and vacuous.

A growth theory, by contrast, means that people explicitly 'express greater interest in new areas'. They know they can, and will, find new things to care about the more they look around. They also anticipate that pursuing interests will sometimes be challenging and can keep up their belief in their passion for a topic even when the going gets tough. So, in turn, they give themselves the opportunities to develop those passions and interests, in sync with how the world works – because challenges are inescapable no matter how much we love something.

The fixed approach implores you to simply 'find your passion' like it's hidden under the sofa. Or to 'do what you love', like there is a fundamental truth about what that is. Or suggests that you can simply click your fingers and it will appear in your life without hurdles or effort. Yet it undermines the likelihood that we will *develop* those very things we are searching so strenuously for.

Work passions are *developed*. They are not 'found'. We are not born with them per se. We can develop new ones again and again through our lives. Some of us start that development earlier, some later in their lives. Some will restart time and time again, turning their hands to multiple careers.

If we aren't spending our days doing something we dreamed of since we were tiny then we are not in some way lacking a core element of the human experience. We are just on a different path, from a different starting point, to developing our passions and interests. And indeed, those passions and interests may themselves only just be coming into existence. How many of us are doing, or will do, jobs that we had no idea existed when we were young? Maybe they straight up didn't exist until a few years ago. This, in turn, means that when (not if) we run into challenges during our development of those passions – it is not an automatic confirmation that we are on the wrong track. **Development of work interests and passion, by definition, takes time. And challenge.**

It is easy to look at someone else's life well-lived, one where passion is seemingly consistently expressed and find yourself lacking. But this is not because there is something wrong with you or that you are devoid of an ability to find this depth of feeling for life. It is because it is much easier to connect these dots backwards – to trace a thread, with hindsight, through someone else's life, and illustrate a story of passion that simply did not exist when it was playing out in real time.

Your dashboard isn't something that has to have been formed in your single-digit years. Your dials don't have to be based on the teenage expectations of your future. The values, goals and priorities that make up your dashboard and the component parts of life that your dials represent can – indeed, should – develop as your life, and your passions, develop. Forwards. Into the unknown. Into the unknowable.

Questions to ask yourself
- Where and how are you giving yourself the opportunity to develop your passions?
- Are you trying new things, while also allowing yourself the time to see whether they could become a passion?

_____

_____

_____

_____

Marie

I'm a GP and I just got accepted on to training to become a specialist in menopause and HRT, which means I will run a clinic in a hospital alongside my GP work. I never would have left medical school thinking I wanted to specialise in this. Hell, I didn't even go into medical school thinking I was going to be a GP. I thought I would become a paediatric surgeon: I did two stints in paeds during medical school. As I went through training it became more and more clear to me that, while I loved paeds, I could grow, and was growing to love other things, and general practice was one of those things. Especially as my father was a gynaecological surgeon, so I had a real sense of what it was like to be in a family where someone was always on call. And, as time went on, I realised that it wasn't what I wanted for my life.

The flip side of being a GP though is that it robs you of a lot of independence in some ways. You need to know a bit about everything. Some people think you know nothing about anything, others think you know

> *everything about everything. So it can always feel like*
> *you are letting someone down. This will be a string to my*
> *bow which is 'mine', and where I get to be a real special-*
> *ist in an area where there is a dearth of provision and a*
> *real need.*

I started this section with a story about my husband, so let me end it with another one.

He works in politics. Not in the kissing babies and debating opponents sense, rather, he is a policy wonk. He writes big, thick, doorstop-weight reports into the machinations of government and how to make it work better.

Today, he came bounding in the front door, all full of beans about a public event he chaired with senior speakers from government and the private sector, discussing how government could do better at buying services from companies. Now, this is obviously not a topic that the younger version of him knew existed, forget about cared for in the way he now does. But it lights him up. He loves the details. He loves marshalling the experts and the practitioners and having something intelligent and impactful to say about an area of government which affects every single one of us.

He only found his way to this area of expertise and the format in which he best enjoys digging into it – writing those reports, speaking to the experts, and forming and sharing opinions – by progressing from job to job through his twenties. Through The Progressively Less Shit Years, from working in Parliament, to one charity and then another; enjoying bits, hating others, thriving in some respects and pottering along in others. Developing his passions.

Your journey to discovering your own passions and interests may well be winding or a little more direct, but it is almost always going to be a journey. Accepting that rather than judging yourself for it is what is going to make that significantly more enjoyable en route.

THE HOW OF WORK

Developing a passion, or many, through the years of your work or the decades of your career is an important piece of the puzzle, but it is not the only piece that matters.

The how of work is a second necessary part of finding career fulfilment.

Even if you're passionate about the 'why' of your job – whether that is saving lives, protecting the environment, creating art or, indeed, wonky UK political topics – there are a million ways to do these things: sitting or standing; talking or typing; alone or with others. We all have preferences, even if they change over time or we are yet to fully nail them down.

Let me give you a real-life example of this. Daisy Buchanan was obsessed with magazines as a girl. She spent years reading and collecting them, poring over the glossy pages night after night after night. This was the world pre-broadband and pre-smartphones – also known as the nineties. Magazines were a big deal.

As she grew up to be a writer, the role she held up as her 'dream job' was to work in-house at a magazine. Years of freelance writing eventually got her there. However, the disconnect between what being a *freelance* writer and a *staff magazine* writer meant stopped her in her tracks. Quite literally.

Daisy soon realised that, despite the obvious pieces of the job being about writing, she didn't account for the fact that, as a freelance writer, she was used to spending 'day after day living in [her] own head', doing her own thing. In the office, she was 'forced to engage with the world. Anyone can ask you anything at any time, and you can't craft your response, as you would on an email – you must go live. Also, you're suddenly not responsible for setting your own workload, so you're always terrified that you're going to get shouted at for not doing enough.'

Months of working in a way that was so out of sync with her preferred way of working meant that her anxiety disorder flared, making her 'cry on waking, before bed, on the bus, in the coffee queue and throughout the credits at a screening of *Pitch Perfect 2*'. Daisy ultimately quit, returned to freelancing writing and is now a full-time, and very successful, author.[5]

So much of 'work' isn't about the job title or the industry or all that, admittedly wonderful, bigger picture stuff; it is about how we spend our days. The in-between moments that make up so much of our jobs, the rhythms of a week and a year. About the how of doing what you do. It is easy to overlook this essential part of finding fulfilment in our careers.

Writing is not one job. And nor is sales, or coding, or cooking, or caring. Or any of a thousand different types of jobs. The how of work matters hugely.

I, for one, hate being cold. As a teenager I did all the usual low-pay jobs (note, decidedly not low-skill, even though I was short of much skill doing them): waitressing, stacking shelves, working on a checkout, and a lot more waitressing. One holiday period from university, I spent my nights refilling the shelves of the local, enormous supermarket. (I apparently failed the psycho-metric tests to get a job on the shop floor during the day. Take from that what you will!)

I didn't mind the repetition of the work itself. There was a satisfying order to it all. I more than didn't mind chatting to my colleague, who would spend the long nights telling me all about her grown-up sons and their various successes in life of which she was so proud. But what I could not handle was the cold. For I was assigned, every night, to the cheese section. Cheddar, Brie, Camembert, the squishy goat's cheese cylinders that dent no matter how gently they are handled – that was my domain.

No matter how many layers I would add under my less-than-fetching uniform, by the time morning came at the end of my night shift, I would be a block of ice. I'd stiffly shuffle my way home, falling into bed as the sun rose, curled up but in such a way so that none of my limbs was touching my body, so frozen were they that I couldn't handle them draining more of my core heat.

Fast-forward 20 years and my guilty work secret is how much I love working in an office where the temperature is steady all year round. Yes, I like to run around the trading floors, football field sized spaces a flight of stairs apart, talking to people in person and clocking up several thousand steps. Add in a commute and, on an ideal day, a walk or two to a client meeting, and I'm happily ticking my smartwatch activity boxes. But, at heart, I am an inside girl basking in my inside life in my nice inside dress and totally-not-waterproof inside shoes. I enjoy tapping on a keyboard plugged into a supersized screen, chatting away on the phone for hours a day. In short, I expressly do not want to face the elements on the daily. I would much rather burn mental energy than physical energy. Even if everything else was the same about my job, I would not do it if it involved being outside all day. Or anywhere near an industrial chiller aisle.

It is not that my supermarket job was not meaningful to me. Those nights were paying for me to live, and party, while I did my university degree. The degree that in turn enabled me to meet the man who would become my husband and get the qualifications I needed to begin the career I now thrive in. But gosh I hated being cold.

My story is a silly one, but it speaks to a bigger point, about people doing much more important things than I ever have, or will do. About the how of work.

The how of work matters hugely. We each need to able to find a *how* of working that suits us. Just as passions are developed, our hows can be too. Through trial and error. Experimenting. Data collection from different jobs, or projects, or companies. Locations, offices, from home or otherwise. Perhaps one of the few silver linings of pandemic working was that you had a chance to experience a different way of working. What does the mechanics of a great day at work look like for you? Not the content, or the achievements, or the benefits. But the raw *how* of it. When you are checking back and forth whether your dials express your dashboard, or whether to remove or add or adjust a dial, have a little sense-check whether it may be *the how* rather than *the what* that is troubling you.

THE BENEFITS OF BOUNDARIES

We've talked about the development of passions. We've talked about working out what the how of work looks and feels like for you. And now I am going to add one final component to the career fulfilment mix.

For the longest time I felt like I was doing work wrong, that I had 'sold out' because I hadn't found an experience from my youth which guided me towards a passion or purpose which I could then turn into a career. That my interests had developed and weren't embryonic businesses in their own rights. We have a culture that tells us office work is bad or boring or that working for 'the man' is inherently unfulfilling. Yet, here's me enjoying it and what it brings to my life. I must be entirely soulless, right? Actually, maybe don't answer that . . .

These worries got louder as I developed other passions in life, like yoga, writing and, most of all, my children. Not from any place inside me, but because so many people quizzed me about them – 'Oh wow, Rebecca, when are you going to go off and be a full-time yoga practitioner/influencer/author/mother?' – hundreds of times over, with the unspoken underlying assumption being: you can't possibly want to do this banking malarkey when you have other options.

Then something pretty wild happened to me after I returned to work after having my first son. Suddenly, work got *more meaningful and more enjoyable.* Even though the development of the passions themselves hadn't changed, nor had the details of the how I was living – or, should I say, working – them. Because I discovered the power of boundaries.

Don't get me wrong, the logistics of a day, of life, were – are – significantly more complex once children are thrown into the mix. Adding the wants and needs of very tiny and very demanding people on to those of bosses and clients and our own ambitions is no small feat. Neither is getting out of bed to face a busy day when you've spent half the night awake. Or rushing home to relieve childcare then getting sucked into a two-hour vortex of dinner, chaos, baths, chaos, stories, chaos, bedtime, chaos, before you even glance up to do the laundry or the work emails or renew the house insurance.

My world post-kids is full of infinitely more love, but also a lot more things to do in a static allotment of time. This creates conflict. Full stop.

But motherhood crystallised for me exactly what work could offer and did contribute and why I *needed* it in my life, as well as what it was never going to be able to provide. Which enabled me, in turn, to put up boundaries around it in a way I never could, or did, in life pre-kids.

I love my career in and of itself. I get a huge amount of personal fulfilment from what I achieve at work. I am energised by what I do there and by the people I get to spend time with because of it. The challenges I have faced, and will continue to face, have enabled quite stunning amounts of personal and professional growth. It sates my never-ending curiosity about the world and about the varying stripes of people within it. I get to hire and train and mentor and sponsor a whole swath of people for whom I know success in the finance industry will be life-changing, and to speak up in rooms that have rarely heard voices like mine, and, in some small ways, make change happen in the world. And it funds a truly wonderful life to boot.

But I also love it precisely because it is *not* my time with my kids. Or time on my yoga mat, or writing a book, or exploring a new city with my husband, or enjoying a glass of wine or two with friends, or just taking a nap on a Sunday afternoon. All things that I get to experience more freely, more deeply and more joyfully because they do not have to provide all the things that work does.

Ingrid
I used to think about work as something negative – something I had to do and would never choose to do. It really surprised me when I decided I wanted to go back to work after I had a baby. I do three days a week now. It's been a real solace, and a place for an essential part of my identity as a creative person.

The primary reason I stopped teaching yoga was that it changed for me when it became work. My yoga practice had been a zero-expectation place, a meditation. Yet when I was teaching a regular class, questions and assessments would pop into my head after, or indeed during, every flow: 'maybe you could put this in next week's class', 'what if those poses got switched, would the flow work better' and on and on.

This is not to say that some people will not find a harmonious way of integrating more of their lives into their work. Or indeed making their lives their work. Social media has done a fantastic job of showing us this approach over the past decade; and what a wonderful additional path it is for some. The travel influencers making holidays into content, or the gaming YouTubers getting paid to play all day, or the fashionistas creating a career out of their daily choices of what to wear.

But the elevation of work above all else – the culture of workism – tells us that everything we do must be in the pursuit of more output. And the siren song of social media can surreptitiously reinforce this message: that work being your actual life and your life being your actual work is the only way of finding ease, or joy, or fulfilment on the career-plus-life front. That many an influencer is now fond of the 'signing off socials for the weekend' post on a Friday night shows that even those who do social media professionally are aware of the dangers of this boundary-loosening reality.

It is a counter-intuitive truth that parenthood can make work easier in this way. It is the first time for many of us that we have a non-negotiable that allows us to firstly create these boundaries and then secondly experience their radiating positive benefits. Motherhood has helped me put up boundaries around my work, and both *my work and I* have thrived because of it.

The expectation that 'work' is one singular thing which should provide everything that is special and meaningful to us, on top of contributing to the world and keeping our families clothed and fed and entertained, is a terrifyingly high bar to set.

When you start creating and embracing these boundaries, you can begin to treasure work for whatever it brings to your life. Work doesn't have to be flawless, like the 'find your passion' or 'follow your dreams' simplifications hint it should be. Work 'just' has to perform the role that it needs to at this point in your life. Be that income. Or learning. Or a stepping-stone to something else. Or a blend of several things. But never, ever, is it everything. Therefore, again, I will encourage you to have more than one work- or career-related dial on your dashboard. This can really help to pull apart the different things that matter to you and the different ways you are expending effort on those priorities or needs. The specific job you have right now is not the same thing as your overall career. A project you are working on, or a client you are trying to secure, or a promotion you are aiming for can be separate to your job, or indeed your career. And all these things are, in turn, separate and distinct from the rest of your life and your identity as a person. Important, yes. Discrete, absolutely. **Boundaries between ourselves and our work, boundaries between the component pieces of work and career – this is how we can appreciate our work for what it is and what it contributes, not what it is lacking.**

Take a second here and think about the roles that work needs to or can perform for you. Think about the boundaries that do, or perhaps do not (yet), exist between these different dials of your work life and all the other dials of your life. While the obvious boundaries – like getting out of the office, or stepping away from your laptop at a sensible time, or taking proper holidays – are all essential, of course, they are the bare minimum. I am talking about something deeper than that: a boundary of not expecting your current job to be all things to you; about giving yourself the time to turn up the other dials in your life.

Hannah

When I was in the military, it was easier in many ways to have ideological boundaries because it was about me fitting into the box of military life that had nothing to do with me as an individual. Wear the uniform, live on the base they tell you, go on deployment. Now I've created this unique and bespoke life and career, it's totally my own box, which is wonderful. But when something work-wise doesn't take off in the way I hoped, it feels a lot more personal.

The things I get meaning from outside of work are even more important to me now – the other dials of friendship, my partner, time in nature, dance and my personal development (I love to do courses and work with coaches).

Embracing the boundaries between the various elements of our work and everything else in our lives enables us to enjoy the best of each of them. Embracing the distinctness of your dials as exactly that – separate, independent component parts – can enable a fulfilled career and life.

Chapter 9

THE TRADES OF LIFE

GETTING IN A black cab for a personal journey never gets old for me – the frivolousness of it; the London-ness of it; the bouncing around in the back seat around the back streets; the thrill and privilege of getting delivered exactly where you need to be via a magical route no one else seems to know exists.

As I was getting started on this chapter, I had a meeting with my editor. It was at the publisher's offices, a beautiful glass-fronted riverside building in central London. I was running late from a client meeting so hopped in a black cab in Mayfair. Bob's black cab to be exact.

Bob asked me whether I was going back to work, and soon I was explaining all things about this book and my full-time career as an investment banker, plus sprinklings about yoga and kids and the like.

We batted back and forth about life and work, and he began to tell me about how he had managed his own. He was bursting with pride to share that his 18-year-old daughter had just secured a role at a very swanky London hotel. And, without skipping a beat, he told me how he had switched his driving hours to drop her off and pick her up at the beginning and ends of her shifts, which sometimes ran very early into the morning or very late at night.

I commented how lovely that was and how lucky she must feel. He shooed my sentiments away, saying it was just the latest version of what he'd always done: when his daughter was small, he'd worked night shifts for many years so he could take his wife to work and his kids to school every weekday morning.

'You make it all sound so simple!' I said.

Bob laughed, glancing at me in the rear-view mirror as he deftly navigated the back streets behind Pall Mall.

'I'm skipping over the tough bits of course,' he said, smiling, before going on to detail the years of broken sleep and the impact on his health and family finances.

There wasn't an ounce of doubt in Bob's mind, though, that he had made the right decisions for him and his family, from those that were available to him. But they were, are, still very real 'trades' all the same: things he and his family gained – time together, mutual support, the ease that brought to all their lives – for things they went without, such as sleep, health and more income.

This perfectly encapsulates the value exchange of work. And, indeed, the trades of life. **How we express the values, goals and priorities of our dashboards as our own set of dials is, by definition, a series of choices. And choices mean trades.** I am using the word 'trade' here, deliberately, rather than 'trade-off'. 'Off' suggests a loss or a downgrade, and that is not what a trade has to be. A trade in its purest sense is a simple exchange – one thing for another. A trade can – indeed, should – be win–win. You give something that is of less value *to you* and receive in exchange something of greater value. Yes, many of these decisions are not going be taken lightly, and we are likely to have some feelings about the path not taken – some strong feelings! – but that doesn't mean we have lost something in making the trade we have. This is the human condition: to live one life in one direction, forwards, and have to make a tonne of choices along the way about that. We should be much more explicit and open about the trades we are making which are inherent in that, but it doesn't mean we have to feel loss around them.

There are countless ways of expressing a value like 'kindness', or a goal like 'financial stability', or a priority like 'family'. Some people will have more options available for them to do so, some fewer. But none of us, none, can choose *all* versions simultaneously. There are choices, and there will be trades that come with the version you end up with. Hopefully by choice; however, sometimes not. And an honest and frank discussion of the reality of those trades can, I hope, help each of us make better ones.

Emelia

I've been able to entirely structure my work around being there every day for my two kids because I work for myself. I do all the drops-offs and pick-ups. The trade is that when I do the pick-up my working day hasn't ended. I can be shushing the kids if I have to take a call or I am the mum typing out an email at the school gates. I was back working four days a week after my daughter was born. My kids get my presence a lot more, but they don't always get all of me. This works for me and I think – know – it works for them. I can always be there when they are ill or when they are hitting a milestone. I might just then be working until 3am to catch up.

WORK IS VALUE EXCHANGE

Work is not your entire identity or your only way of defining yourself, as we established in Chapter 7. It should not be a boundary-less gifting of effort outwards, as we discussed in Chapter 8. Yes, we might love it (sometimes, often ... maybe even always). But we should be getting something valuable in return: the compensation, or the impact, or the learning, or the creativity, or the service, or whatever the mix is for each of us at any given time or in any given job.

The usual tropes of 'work–life balance', or 'having it all, just not at the same time', or 'having anything you want, but not everything you want', or 'find your passion' glaze over all of this. They ignore the reality that there are truly no cost-free decisions. That what we are really deciding when we make a choice, from good options or from bad, is the specific type of suffering we would prefer. I am adapting these words from philosopher Alain de Botton's musings on marriage as they apply so well to another long-term relationship: work.[1] Because suffering comes for us all, at some point. Just in many differing forms, and during the inevitable ups and downs on every path. Ultimately, **a life of ease isn't about things being easy, it's about choosing the struggles that suit us best, if and where we can.**

Yet how often do we hear it framed this way? How often do we get honest and transparent conversations and assessments of the various trades every single person is making when it comes to work and life?

Bob took me through some of the trades he has made and many of the component parts of his trades will feature in our own – things like pay and flexibility. But there are many more likely parts of likely trades. Like benefits. Like status. Like exposure to or protection from discrimination. Things like hours. Control. Values.

Mission. Certainty. Creativity. Impact. Ownership. Optionality for the future. Content of the work itself.

A business owner might be trading hours (lots and lots and lots) for the chance to hit the big time or because they want the control that being in charge brings. Which itself is a huge, immovable, responsibility.

An influencer might be trading formal benefits (none), certainty (little), for creativity (lots), flexibility (acres) and status (cool factor off the charts!).

A doctor might be trading hours (lots) and flexibility (little), for mission (nothing higher), status (again, saint-like) and impact (unfathomable).

A journalist might be trading hours (lots) and pay (little) for status and mission (plenty of each).

Are they exchanges you would make? Possibly, probably not. Are they exchanges everyone can make? Definitely not. Because while there is always a trade, the choices available to each of us vary endlessly and are not fairly distributed. Definitely not at any given time, and possibly even at any time. Yet whatever options are available, whatever mix you choose, there *will* be a trade. Something you get, for something you give away.

What we are aiming for here is the *lowest cost* trade for each of us. Not sure what that is for you? Your dashboard is the touchstone to keep coming back to: if it truly matters to you, it should be on there. Your dials are the real-life feedback mechanism on trades: does the option you are contemplating mean turning a dial to an unacceptable level or removing it entirely? How does that stack against your dashboard values, priorities and goals? The answers to all of these questions can and should change through the many seasons of life. But there is invariably a trade, and acknowledging it explicitly is much more likely to bring to you a sense of peace with that truth.

I sometimes look at my husband and think I want to have kids the way he does. All the genetic connection, and six months of shared parental leave, and the joys of raising them, but none of the physical exhaustion of repeated pregnancies, the injuries of birth or the months of breastfeeding, just for a start.

The physical 'having' of the babies is the first thing we've done in our relationship that hasn't been 'fair'. When we found out at our 12-week scan for our second pregnancy that I had a so-called missed miscarriage (this is where the baby stopped developing several weeks earlier but my body had continued the rest of the pregnancy without recognising it), I remember sobbing gently in the scanning room – now I would have to go through various horrible procedures and experiences only to, hopefully, do another first trimester. All just to get back to where I thought I was before we walked into that room.

It was a cruel reality, but an unavoidable one for us. All the while knowing that, as awful as it was, we were still going through this despair with incredible good fortune on our side: a two-year-old at home; knowledge we could, and did, get pregnant more than once; a wonderful NHS to pick up the pieces; and – more on this later – a wonderfully supportive work set-up which meant I could, and did, entirely turn my work dial to zero for the time I needed to.

I am the only one in this relationship who gets to physically have the babies. That itself is a gift. And it is a burden. Pregnancy is not a health-neutral event. Pregnancy in our current societal structure is not a life-neutral event. This truth factored into a multitude of decisions and trades I have made about my career path and priorities. I knew that if we wanted biological children, it was going to involve me being pregnant and birthing them. And I would need a lot of support around me to do so. Full stop.

Forget about if I wanted to enjoy, or dare I even say thrive in, the process.

These are inescapable realities for most heterosexual women. In the summer of 2022, the tennis superstar Serena Williams announced her retirement from the sport. Her statement, printed in *Vogue*, is a moving read – her love for tennis, for her daughter, for her new venture capital business. She explains how, ultimately, she needed to choose between tennis and a family. She wants another child and 'cannot be' pregnant again as an athlete. 'I need to be two feet into tennis or two feet out,' she explains. Going on to say, 'I don't think it's fair. If I were a guy, I wouldn't be writing this because I'd be out there playing and winning while my wife was doing the physical labour of expanding our family. Maybe I'd be more of a Tom Brady if I had that opportunity.'[2]

Though women are the ones who face the physical trades more than men, it is not just women who face career versus family trades.

Just a few days after Williams' retirement announcement, came one from another sporting great: Sebastian Vettel, the Formula One Driver and multiple world champion. He explained his choice to step away from the sport thus: 'Committing to my passion the way I did and the way I think is right, no longer goes side-by-side with my wish to be a great father and husband. The energy it takes to become one with the car and the team, to chase perfection, takes focus and commitment. My goals have shifted from winning races and fighting for championships to seeing my children grow, passing on my values, helping them up when they fall, listening to them when they need me, not having to say goodbye, and most importantly being able to learn from them and let them inspire me.'[3]

There are very real trades we all have to make at different points in our lives and careers. Some biologically dictated, some not. And these examples are fairly non-controversial ones because they are rooted in 'good' choices.

Gender pay gaps, or racial disparities in hiring practices, or the prevalence of the motherhood penalty, or the precariousness of zero-hour contracts, or the gulf in pay rates between key workers and commercial professions, or the availability of financing to different groups of business owners . . . these all speak to realities in the world that will leave many with a series of bad options to 'choose' from or trade. For example, the single parent faced with the decision between taking extra training that could ultimately lead to a better paid career path, but in the short term will give them less time with their children and much greater pressures of running life, is stuck between a rock and a hard place.

A fantastic, if faintly depressing, *Vanity Fair* article catalogues the trials of the new swath of journalists and writers who have gone independent and now offer their wares via platforms such as Substack.[4] In the piece, they describe how they've effectively swapped one set of anxieties for another, worrying about keeping up their publishing cadence and whether it's fair to their subscribers to take holiday, instead of how well they are performing against other salaried writers and whether they'll get sacked.

Independence has value *and* cost. It is a trade. A good one for some. A bad one for others.

The market has a wildly different way of assigning earning capacity to different jobs. Different jobs and careers and paths will come with wildly different types of 'benefits', like flexibility or paid leave or fun staff retreats or the ability to work from the beach. Society has a wildly different way of assigning other types of value too: prestige, power, status, control. Backgrounds and networks and a stunningly complicated matrix of other factors all contribute to the reality of the choices we can make on the work and career front. The vast majority of which won't be strictly fair.

And therein lies a crucial calculation that each of us must make when it comes to the value exchange of work, and the trades of life: what are we going to trade for, and what are we going to trade away?

Questions to ask yourself

- What are your dashboard priorities and dials that work must contribute to?
- What is the work available to you to achieve these?
- How can you leverage your skills, education, network or other factors to access this?
- What could or will change in the future?

_____

_____

_____

_____

SHARING MY TRADES

I wish I could give the perfect run-down for people in all the careers, from all walks of life, from all different bodily, cultural and social advantages and disadvantages. But that would be an encyclopaedia in and of itself and still likely fail to cover the unique mix of you, your life and your circumstances.

What I can do is this: share my story, the rationale that went into my decisions and some of the data and research that exists to contextualise that. As well as ask you to consider your own trades, and ask others about theirs. This is not about whether you would make my precise trades, but to identify the trades _you_ are willing and able to make, given your dashboard and dials. Because there is, *always*, a trade – between or in the where, how and what to do with work, with careers, with everything else in your life.

What helps precisely no one is pretending any of this does not exist. Or that there is a zero-cost option. There is *always* utility to be found in acknowledging the situation as it is, before we then begin to change it.

Money versus risk versus passions

I have made a trade to prioritise earning. It feels somewhat uncouth to say that out loud, which is why so few people do, but it is true. I am grateful every single day that I did. It has brought, and bought, so much to my life that would not have been available to me by any other route.

The flip side of that trade has been thus. In getting this level of earnings, I gave away vast swaths of my twenties. I got up at 5am and was in the office before 6am, leaving 12–14 hours later, on a good day. For years I worked on weekends, over Christmas, on New Year's Day. I said no to anything, everything, which got in the way, including sleep and travel and hobbies and fitness and time with the people I love.

What is also true on the money front is that I have prioritised a lower risk, lower potential reward way of earning at the higher end of the scale. The way to the biggest pay-off is to own a business. Data out of the US shows that there are three times as many business owners among the top brackets of earners as those who are there due to their wages.[5] The Berkeley professors behind the research address this point explicitly: 'in both number and aggregate income, [business owners] far surpass that of top public company executives'.

The real choice for the absolute highest possible income is not the path I have chosen.

I knew from the first day I walked into my graduate position, that if I could hang on to a job, it would be well paid. I knew that there would be rungs to climb and promotions to get and that there would almost always be a job for me in some shape or form in the industry. There is a level of certainty in a corporate path. And certainty is an important value on my dashboard. I was, am, simply not willing to roll the dice of building and running a business. It is significantly more risk, uncertainty and uncontrollable hours than the wage route . . . in my book at least.

To suggest that anyone or everyone could simply choose to work in a very high-pay industry is to offensively ignore truths about access, at a minimum. Yet there are trades many of us will be making between industries and companies and career paths that maximise or minimise key features, like pay.

These careers are not as available as they should be, but nor are they as closed as many expect. And even relatively junior people, or those in the less glamorous parts of the finance sector, can earn well over six figures.

There are many of us for whom jobs entail managing people or processes and projects, or doing HR, or writing reports and so on. If the *content* the process relates to isn't one of your dials, why not optimise for something that is? Perhaps it is money. Perhaps it is mission. Perhaps it's the chance to be outside all day rather than in an office building. An HR job at an investment bank is going to pay a lot more than at a charity. A data analytics role in the civil service is going to come with a lot more social mission than the stock options the same role might generate at a fintech start-up. Here we are again with the trades.

On a personal level, the content of my work is low value to me. I enjoy the 'getting it done' aspect of what I do, but it is not hugely relevant whether the 'it' I am doing relates to financial markets or widgets or wormholes. Content isn't one of my dials and I have turned that to my advantage by going broader in my career as I've climbed the ladder. Rather than being a specialist, I can and do pick up a wide variety of topics on any given day, month or year.

I have made a trade that gets me more money, for less risk, for less obvious passionate content.

Given your dashboard and dials, what are the trades that you would make?

> **Joel**
> *The whole point in going into this field was because I felt strongly about the topics I am working on. Even within my broad career path, there are ways I could have gone to maximise my income or responsibility – mostly going to work for an agency or in-house for a corporate or running a team. I haven't done that. I never wanted to be a gun-for-hire or to manage lots of people. I want to be a subject matter expert. The trade is that progression gets more limited from here. Again, I don't want to manage, so it's not a difficult one for me.*

Support versus control

I have explicitly and repeatedly optimised for support in my career and traded away elements of control in exchange.

Some of that support looks like multiple paid maternity leaves and acres of paid holiday time, and what I would describe as a more dialable career path in the years when I needed it to be. I have, on multiple occasions, some happy, some less so, been able to dial my work dial right down with little or no effect on my career path or earnings because I am working for a huge firm with huge resources: the happy times of having babies, or going on yoga teacher-training, or just a kick-ass multi-week road trip with my husband; the less happy times of serious ill health, family emergencies and a miscarriage.

Being replaceable can feel like vulnerability at many points in a corporate career, but it is also the thing that means you do not have to trade your very existence for your work. Yes, I did the crazy work in my youth, but I do not do it now. Working for a large, market-leading corporate, for me, has provided so much of the resilience factor that we discussed in Chapter 5. That experience showed me, real time, that it suits me and my preferences, or lack thereof, for risk; how much I value the large solid infrastructure of a large solid organisation; and how much I value the support of a fleet of people whose pay cheques do not rely on my ability to never need to stop working.

The flip side of this is that I march to the beat of the firm, my bosses, my team, my clients and the global financial markets. I work from the office most days, even though one COVID-related silver lining is more acceptance about working from home. Still, the truth is that it is easier for me to do my job from the trading floor than not.

While I am now senior enough to move my hours around so my daily dedicated time with my kids is protected no matter what, I still relatively frequently end up on calls at 11pm responding to a client issue. I keep an eye on my inbox whether I am working or not, and would always rather get a call from a client who needed me on my holiday or over the weekend than pick up the pieces when I am more officially back at work.

I'm a mother *and* I'm a fixer, so days where I am needed on both fronts bring me a lot of joy. So, the support-for-control trade is a decidedly low-cost trade for me, but still, it is very much a trade.

Another dimension of the support versus control trade relates to discrimination.

Various forms of legislation exist in most countries to limit both the existence and impact of various types of discrimination. In the UK, the Equality Act of 2010 replaced various statutes from the prior decades, covering nine protected qualities (age, disability, gender reassignment, marriage or civil partnership, pregnancy and maternity, race, religion or belief, sex and sexual orientation).[6] Similar legislation applies in the EU, and to some extent in the US.[7]

However, there remain some fundamental flaws in these protections. Firstly, that legislation often does not protect the population in a uniform way. The self-employed are not protected from being unfairly dismissed from work. They have no legal rights to sick pay or maternity/paternity/adoption leave and pay. And, secondly, the legislation often fails to even do what it says on the tin. Less than 1 per cent of victims of pregnancy or maternity discrimination in the UK take legal action against a discriminatory employer for example.[8] And that discrimination can happen anywhere. Activist Joeli Brearley, founder of the campaigning organisation Pregnant Then Screwed, catalogues in her book, *The Motherhood Penalty,* examples of women discriminated against by the Ministry of Justice, Network Rail, care homes, a women's organisation, a school, a coffee chain, the European Commission, a recruitment company, and more.[9]

I was shocked when in a pregnancy announcement post, one of my favourite fashion/motherhood/interiors influencers told of how she had kept this, her second, pregnancy firmly under wraps for many additional months versus her first.[10] Because when she broke the news of being pregnant that first time, virtually all the brands she was working with had simply dropped her, saying that they 'couldn't' work with her while she was pregnant. Literally, in writing. She learned through conversations in the months and years that followed that the various brands were concerned that pregnant women weren't 'relatable', and that it would suggest the fashion brand had or was a maternity line, or that the skincare was specifically catering for pregnancy-related issues. She couldn't earn any money for five months of her pregnancy, which then ended in unpaid maternity leave. As such, she started working again five weeks after her son was born.

This is just one form of discrimination. Sexism, racism, classism, homophobia, and more, are pervasive too.

In the past few days of writing this chapter, an investigation at a very well-known cancer charity found significant amounts of racist and ableist discrimination.[11] An academic paper was published showing that women in scientific research teams are significantly less likely to be credited with authorship than men.[12] A survey conducted by the Chartered Management Institution showed that 71 per cent of employees from a Black background reported feeling overlooked for opportunities owing to their identity, as did 65 per cent of those who identified as LGBTQ+.[13] This is all from a random, single-digit day period.

This shit (and it is shit) is everywhere. It will vary across industries and companies and be minimised by the amazing bosses and maximised by the horrific ones.

While a big corporate life is far from perfect, it often can provide more protection than many other paths and set-ups. Guided by the knowledge that certainty is an important value on my dashboard, a piece of the trade I have made is for the more explicit relative protections of a large, high-profile corporate. I appreciate, and benefit from, the fact that standards of behaviour are higher in formalised work and hyper-commercial organisations that are competing for talent left, right, and centre. I give back something control-wise in exchange.

Luca

The best thing about working for myself is that I get to choose what I say yes to, both in terms of the work I do and the people I do it with, and the day-to-day rhythms of how I want to work. This means I can keep non-work dials that are important to me like my health, time in nature and the various classes I take consistently turned up more than when I had a traditional career. The trade is that I have to do it all: I have to create the big-picture strategy, as well as all the detailed plans, and then I have to go out and do it all. I was good at managing a team when I did it and I miss having that camaraderie and people who could pick things up and run with them. It's been an adjustment.

More versus less

Some portion of the trades I have already mentioned are only made possible because I have a spouse who is willing and able to pick up the home-life pieces. One who has taken six months' shared parental leave alongside me, twice, despite not getting paid for it – a privilege afforded to us by my pay, and a reflection of how we approach both money and parenting in our relationship. But still, a massive privilege that many men, or families, cannot afford, due in no small part to the discrimination against them in paternity pay.

This is increasingly, however, what partnership must look like in a world of 'greedy' work.[14] This term describes the current reality of many professions where workers get paid proportionally more for the more hours put in. Not just that people who do these demanding jobs earn more in total as they work more, but that they *get paid more on a per hour basis* as they work increased hours.

Harvard economist Claudia Goldin's stunning book *Career and Family* illuminates the past 100-odd years of female access to and assent in the labour force in the US. She shows how the value of greedy jobs has 'soared' since the eighties: 'jobs with the greatest demands for long hours and the least flexibility have paid disproportionately more, while earnings in other employments have stagnated'.[15]

Saying this another way: firms pay much more to those who work in the least flexible positions. This is greedy work. This is a 'day job' dial which is harder to turn down exactly when you choose. This is a money dial that is often harder to turn up, because that flexibility costs workers. Add gender norms on too and more women than men take, prioritise or are routed into the more flexible paths, even though, now more than ever, women *and* men want both careers *and* to actively participate in raising a family.[16]

With greedy work, comes couple inequity. The 50-50 couple might be happier, but it would be significantly poorer. In a world where the price of couple equity is too high and the difference in earnings between two jobs is substantial 'the average couple will opt for higher family income and often, to their mutual frustration and sorrow, will thereby be forced to throw gender equality and couple equity under the bus'.[17]

My husband's choice to reduce his working days while we shielded for the last months of my pregnancy was itself an illustration of this, and a piece of the trade I, we, have made. The decision itself was a rushed one, made at midnight on Sunday night after a cancelled Christmas and news of increasingly horrific outcomes of the Beta COVID strain on pregnant women, particularly those with histories of blood clots and lung damage – boxes I ticked. We needed to shield. And we needed me to work. My bosses and colleagues and clients were endlessly supportive, but

I knew I was a few months away from turning my work dial right down while on maternity leave, and I needed to make those months prior to that point count.

My husband stepped back so I didn't have to because the pay-offs of that for us as a family were so significant.

In some ways, Goldin got the couple inequity point spot-on: due to my 'greedy work', we moved from both working full-time and parenting equally, to one person working less and parenting more. However, we did this the unusual way around. He stepped back, I stayed working. It is not just unusual from a pure gender play, but it is unusual from a pay perspective too: studies show that even when the woman in a heterosexual relationship is earning more, she is still more likely to sacrifice paid work once the couple become parents.[18]

There is a societal default: man works more; woman cares more. Because our familial default does not match this, it renders explicit between us what would otherwise be implicit. Because we are going against the grain, the friction makes what would otherwise be unconscious totally visceral. Rather than assuming that I, as a woman, will be the lead parent, we make more conscious, deliberate, and I believe equitable, decisions.

Consistently taking shared parental leave is a piece of that. Affordable for us due to my greedy work, my husband's leave was largely unpaid (like most of the parental leave for fathers in the UK. Explaining a piece of why take-up rate among eligible dads in the UK in 2019 was just 3.6 per cent).[19] And we make numerous other day-to-day and longer-term decisions that reflect our commitment to equality in our relationship and in our parenting.

But still, I am, we are, making trades here. I am trading more hours worked for less time with my family. There is no escaping the raw maths of this right now. That temporal qualifier is, I hope, an important one. The disproportionate pay-offs of greedy work mean, again I hope, that this won't be the trade I make for the entirety of my children's years at home. The trades my husband and I are making between his and my careers we plan, again, to be temporal: my work dial is turned up more than his right now but won't be forever. Equally, he's dialled up his time with our kids, but it won't be his 'turn' forever. There is a lot of more versus less going on for both for us as individuals, and between us in our marriage and as parents.

YOUR TRADES

Ultimately, my trades have been for less small 'f' flexibility: not being able to totally control my hours or working location, for more big 'F' Flexibility: paid maternity leave, paid holiday and sick leave, and a multitude of other benefits of working for a big corporate, including a ream of formal and informal protections against discrimination. They have been high, stable income, and all the ease and resilience that brings to my life. For high pressure, and working evenings and weekends when needed. And less time with my kids, right now, than my husband (or my nanny), but a world away from the weekend warrior parent that seemed to be the only option when I got into the industry in the late noughties.

I've traded ownership for certainty. I've traded the opportunity to work at the higher end of mission and creativity for spending my days knee-deep in highly technical content. I've opted to work in a still heavily male-dominated industry, with the challenges that brings, because it's where I could get rewarded, fast.

These are my trades. They might not be the trades that many others are willing, or able, to make. But I would make every single one of them again.

The key takeaway from this chapter is not whether you would

make the trades I have, or even whether you could. But that you will be, likely already are, making your very own trades. And failing to acknowledge that makes getting them more right, harder. *For everyone.*

Many of the trades we make are going to be influenced and affected by big, impersonal societal trends and truths that we each have little to no control over. There is no cost-free decision. Yet we each must make a trade, a decision, all the same. And the more honest, the more transparent, more of us can be about the trades we have made and why, the more likely we are to make both the best and the least worse ones for us, and change some of the component parts of the equation. Can you think of some trades you have already made? Perhaps one which was so low-cost to you that it barely seems to qualify as one. Or another which still stings slightly; that was harder to weigh up, but the right one? There are likely to be some that more than stung, perhaps even some you ultimately changed course on. My hope is that the answers here show a strong relation to what is on your dashboard and what is coming through in your dials.

Questions to ask yourself

- Is there a decision you are weighing up in life right now?
- What are the gives and takes on each side of the trade that it represents?
- How do they relate back to your dashboard goals, values and priorities?

_____

_____

_____

_____

These are not easy questions. The answers are often even harder. But the more these very real trades get discussed, in the open – significantly more and with significantly more honesty – the less difficult they will get.

Safiya

I retrained as a therapist once my kids were in senior school. It was a total pivot for me and a three-year degree, so a hell of a lot of work. The responsibility is huge. Every patient contact matters. It can really eat you up if you think you've handled something wrong. I need to be on the ball and present with my patients every time I see them and I do little things to ensure that is the case – like I don't drink the days before I am working anymore, or even really do anything in the evenings except go to a workout class. These things aren't sacrifices for me at all, but it is a different life to when I was going out with clients several nights a week and living that PR and marketing lifestyle, or when I could always say yes to friends who wanted to meet up. And, frankly, all that came with earning more money too. I was the bread-winner then; I'm not anymore. That has changed the balance between me and my partner. I couldn't have retrained without his support, but similarly he couldn't have got where he has without me doing the lion's share of the work when the kids were small.

We need to hear from all sorts of people, in all sorts of careers, in all sorts of walks of life discussing the trades they have made. Ask your friends, ask your colleagues, ask your boss. Ask your parents and your grandparents. Ask your interviewer at the next job you are seeking.

And let's stop asking high-profile women how they manage their work–life balance. Instead, let's start asking women *and* men about the trades they have made, and are making, in their careers and in their lives.

For now, I can only come back to the truth that **there are no easy paths or hurdle-free routes on the career fulfilment journey. There are only trades after trades after trades.**

Whether you are on the trading floor, or not.

Chapter 10

MONEY MATTERS

'RRRRRRREBECCA.'

My father's voice echoed up the stairs.

He had been beavering away on the family desktop computer all day. And now I was either in trouble or he wanted me to do something for him. I started weighing up the various possibilities in my head. Given that it was the school Christmas holidays and it was blowing an icy gale outside, being in trouble seemed preferable to having to run an errand at the parade of shops a little walk away. Maybe. Maybe not . . .

'I want to show you something,' my father said.

This could still be being in trouble . . . but at least, I thought, I don't have to leave the house.

'Look at this.' He clicked the noisy beige mouse several times to zoom in (this was long before touchscreens) – he is not a keyboard shortcut kind of man.

I peered closer, not sure which one of the hundreds of cells in the Excel spreadsheet before me I was meant to be focusing on.

'One penny,' my dad said. 'That is how much I was "out" on the family budget versus what we spent this year.'

I made all the right appreciative and impressed noises. But as a barely 16-year-old, I failed to grasp the true significance of the achievement: the diligence required to even capture five peoples' worth of spending over a year and the bigger discipline of setting and keeping to a budget at this scale.

My dad would do this, especially at the end of the year – in the final, most expensive month. Spend hours at the computer, poring over spreadsheets, receipts, letters and bills. Take the time to check his projections against the reality. Time to crunch the numbers of every single incoming and outgoing for our family. And this year, he wanted a witness to the mastery of his craft: running his – our – budgeted and true expenditure down, literally, to the penny.

I'd grown up like this. Watching my parents approach all things money with this level of focus. They were never obsessive about it, but always deliberate. There was a quiet, but ever-present dialogue about money and how it both affected and effected our choices and decisions as a family.

There was one story my mother would come back to time and time again – about how her planned years as a stay-at-home mum with me, my brother and my sister before we reached school age came to a premature halt. Because, well, money.

It was 1988 and my parents were in their late thirties. They had cobbled together a deposit for their first flat – a milestone to celebrate, especially with three kids under five at home. But in the three months it took for the paperwork to complete, interest rates climbed from 7 to 13 per cent. The monthly repayments became unaffordable before they even made the first one. Requiring my mum to get work. Immediately.

She was a teacher by trade, but it would take a little time to hustle up a fresh teaching job, even to sign up as a supply teacher given she was, as a military wife, new to the area. So, she got whatever work she could find, quickly. And this time, it was delivering phone books. She spent the next few months of weekends driving house to house, making deliveries, while my dad entertained the little trio of kids at home. All before putting his RAF uniform back on come Monday morning.

Money was never a life-or-death issue growing up. We had, and have, much to be grateful for on this front. But it was also never an ease, which is the case for many others. It was instead a consistent, sobering factor that was so often the stop/go decider on what would happen next.

It also made me somewhat confused about the prevalence of the message that money doesn't make you happy.

THE PRICE OF HAPPINESS

There is an oft-cited piece of academic research – the one that says something like happiness improves with earning more, but only up to $75,000 – that gets trotted out to back up this claim.[1] Written by two Nobel Laureates, it was, and still is, *everywhere.* Characters quote it on TV shows.[2] It was even number 9 on *Time* magazine's 'Top 10 of Everything List' one year.[3]

That $75,000 number is catchy. It's stuck in my head for a decade plus! However, the actual findings of the research are less so.

Kahneman and Deaton's seminal research in fact does not claim that money only buys happiness up to that level. Their work focuses on two aspects of *subjective well-being*: emotional well-being and evaluation of life – the former being tracking of emotions like joy, anger, sadness or anxiety from the previous day; the latter tracking responses to questions like 'How satisfied are you with your life as a whole these days?' on a scale of 0 to 10, where 0 is 'the worst possible life for you' and 10 is 'the best possible life for you'.

Their findings were, in fact, that high income absolutely buys life satisfaction, i.e. getting the best possible life for yourself. What it doesn't do is buy that better daily emotional experience beyond that level. However, not having money – low income – is also 'associated both with low life evaluation' *and* 'low emotional well-being', meaning that money protects your downside on both fronts.

This feels like a very different reading to the one prevalent in popular culture over the past dozen odd years. Furthermore, over those years, a lot more research has confirmed this message. The most compelling of which, in my book at least and this is my book after all, is a paper named thus: 'If money doesn't make you happy then you probably aren't spending it right.'[4] What a title.

The three authors say that the sentiment that 'the things that bring happiness simply aren't for sale' is 'lovely, popular and almost certainly wrong', before drawing on acres of research to boil down eight principles to help people get more happiness for their money. They include things like spending your money on life experiences rather than on tangible things, spending money on lots of small things that bring joy little and often, rather than saving up your money for one large moment of joy, and to spend your money on others, rather than yourself, will bring you more happiness.

Ultimately, they argue, and show, with reams of data and research, that 'money can buy many, if not most, if not all of the things that make people happy, and if it doesn't, then the fault is ours'.

Money solves problems.

When we spend it right.

It is a massively flexible facilitator of resilience.

Those who are better off financially not only live longer, but they also get significantly more healthy years of life: eight to nine more years after fifty than the poorest individuals in the US and in England, according to research published in *The Journals of Gerontology*.[6] They can choose more meaningful leisure activities (so-called 'active' leisure like socialising, exercising, hobbies and volunteering, versus 'passive' activities like napping or watching TV) and, though they often work similar hours to the rest of us, they optimise to have more autonomy in their jobs.[7,8] These are all very much the ingredients of a happy life.

Finances even dictate our self-assessment of how we parent – surely one of the most personal judgements in the world. Pew Research finds that parents who say they live comfortably give themselves higher ratings at how they are doing at raising their kids than those who are living less comfortably, a scale that gets more extreme the closer to having trouble meeting your expenses you are.[9]

Money is a unique tool. It has versatility. It has flexibility. It is the thing that can get you the most of whatever it is you need, with the least friction. Sometimes you need dental work. Other times you need transport to work. It is a totally fungible resource to battle the challenges of scarcity.

'Fungibility' is the ability of a good or asset to be readily interchanged for another of like kind. This has intrinsic value, even if the paper the notes are written on or the screens from which we check our bank balances do not. You cannot easily or instantly exchange a house for anything: in most countries it requires months of legal work at least. You cannot click your fingers and swap your time for the childcare you need this week. You cannot use your happy marriage to put food on the table. **Money has additional value *because* it can do both *all and any* of these things.** And, as such, we need to have it factor into our dials framework. Explicitly and deliberately.

Am I trying to teach you to suck eggs here? Making an argument that doesn't need to be made? Of course everyone knows having money is important. And, for most of us, that means earning it.

Well, yes and no.

The data shows that pay has been a less important component of the decision-making process for many people over the last couple of decades. A recent (post-pandemic) survey by Deloitte found that pay is the top reason why Gen Zs (those born between 1997 and 2012) and Millennials (those born between 1981 and 1996) left a role in the previous two years.[10] Clearly money matters.

Yet, the same survey showed that, when looking for new jobs, money wasn't the top priority for a significant proportion of respondents. Good work–life balance and learning and development opportunities were key, for both cohorts. And, more than that, high salary or other financial benefits were less important to the younger generation (Gen Zs) than the older (my own, Millennials), coming in as the top response for just 24 per cent of Gen Zs, versus 27 per cent of Millennials. This was even though almost half of those surveyed live pay cheque to pay cheque and worry they won't be able to cover their expenses, and that more than a quarter of Gen Zs and nearly a third of Millennials are not confident they will be able to retire comfortably. This isn't some small-fry survey: Deloitte have been conducting it for over 10 years, in the last round collecting results from over 23,000 people in 46 countries across North America, Latin America, Western Europe, Eastern Europe, the Middle East, Africa and Asia-Pacific.

There is a lot of disconnect represented in this data. A whole lot. And I can't help but think it links back to two truths that sit awkwardly together: that we are, quite rightly, deeply, and perhaps even innately, aware of the damage that money being a goal in and of itself can, will and does do. While knowing that it is no longer a given that generational improvements in income or wealth are coming.

In the US, more than 90 per cent of children born in the forties grew up to earn more than their parents. Today, only half of children will cross that threshold.[11]

In Chapter 8, I mentioned my holiday job stacking cheese through the night at a local supermarket to pay my way through my university degree. It is easy to let a truth that sentence contains slip by, unacknowledged. That, then, it was possible to pay for university by stacking shelves.

UK university tuition fees were capped at £1,000 per year when I started university in 2004. They increased to £3,000 the year I left – 2007. Given that university had been entirely free just six years earlier, I had felt naively jaded about paying fees at all, especially that extra £2,000. Until three years later when the cap was lifted to £9,000.

Taking all the loans I could and working to save during my holidays – waitressing, stacking shelves and then my first jobs in investment banking – meant I could pay the fees, my rent, my living expenses and refill my overdraft by the end of every summer holiday. In the end, I left university with £10,000 of student loans, and a not dissimilar amount of cash saved. No small feat, which contained no small amount of effort and focus. But the same effort and focus just a few years later would not have balanced the same scale.

Even the jobs I was able to take reflected a level of privilege not available to everyone: my parents lived a commutable distance to London, making that first banking internship possible without paying for housing or food. I lived in an easier time, in an easier situation.

Options to earn our way out of money troubles or scarcity are stunningly unequally distributed. These structural factors are massive. And, for many, irrespective of effort or ability or skill, these will be, to some extent or another, insurmountable. Nothing I am saying here removes that truth.

However, we did spend the entire previous chapter talking about trades. You, me, we are each going to be making some decisions about whether, or what, or how, money is or is not a priority in our lives. All amid the very real, very present structural realities in which we exist. We are all likely to be short of important things at various times in our lives. If and when we have some choice about what those things are, I am arguing to do what you can to make it *not money*.

One way we can each do this is to have *at least* one money dial on our dashboards. Money needs to be considered as a standalone component part of your life.

The way you prioritise and adjust your approach to money needs to exist independently of your work and your career. Yes, it can sit next to them in a grouping, but it is separate. Because, while these things are linked for most of us, they are not *the same*. Sometimes work is for skills, sometimes your career is for contributing. Other times it is for the cold, hard cash. But you *always* need to be thinking about money independently. Even if you have so much that all you need to think about is giving it away.

Have a money dial. Have a savings dial. Have an investment dial. Have a donating dial (much more on this in the next chapter). Have one, have three, have others that represent what this topic means to you. Flip back to your dashboard for a second. There might be some more implicit money-related requirements to other aspects of your dashboard that need teasing out and setting up as their own dials here.

Questions to ask yourself

- Does living in a particular location require a financial threshold to be met?
- Does setting up your own business require you to raise some funding, or minimise your household outgoings to enable you to take the leap?

_____

_____

_____

_____

Kat

My money focus is getting rid of the last of my credit card debt. I'm not a natural saver – hence getting into this in the first place. But getting out of it, nearly, has shown me that I can do something consistently positive when it comes to money. Maybe I'll add a savings dial once I get to take this debt-free dial off my dashboard.

Consciously thinking about when and how to move the levels on these dials up and down is, of course, an essential part of this. There are times when it is easier to get or do that high-paying job. There are other times when it makes sense to reduce your savings and spend: a trip of a lifetime, a house renovation, helping a friend in need. There will be moments when you can divert funds into a riskier project, and other times when surprise bills or expenses come along and consume every penny. **Dials are meant to be adjusted.**

Money matters. More than we acknowledge. More than we talk about.

> **Deepak**
> *I'm aware at the moment of the power money has to buy freedom. My wife and I were recently told that we will likely need IVF if we want to have biological children. It is a real blow to realise that doing something which is 'free' for so many people will likely cost us a lot of money.*

As well as making money a more explicit part of your Dials framework, there are some money truths that should be acknowledged too – ones that instead get lost in the general awkwardness about talking about the topic entirely. Let's dive into those now . . .

EARN MORE, EARLY

The pound or dollar or euro you earn at 16 or 21 or 25 is worth more than the one you earn at 35. Or 45. Or 65. A *lot* more.

There are plenty of financial terms that describe this phenomenon – the time value of money, compound interest, exponential growth – but the best way to understand it is to run the maths.

Scenario 1: The monthly squirrel

Imagine that you are a diligent and consistent saver. That consistency is your superpower and you are going to tuck away the same number every month, invest it in an equity index tracker and leave it alone until you retire aged 65.

The equity index tracker piece is important: the average annualised return for the S&P500 (an index of 500 leading, publicly traded US companies) since its inception in 1926 through to the end of 2021 is 10.49 per cent.[12] Even taking a shorter time horizon, since 1957 when the index became 500 strong, it is 10.67 per cent.

At what ages would you have to start this monthly saving and investing strategy for your investment pile to reach a nice round, life-changing number of £1,000,000 by the time you turned 65?

Here are seven examples:[13]

1. Invest £105 every month from age 21.
2. Invest £159 every month from age 25.
3. Invest £265 every month from age 30.
4. Invest £455 every month from age 35.
5. Invest £755 every month from age 40.
6. Invest £2,420 every month from age 50.
7. Invest £4,900 every month from age 60.

Take a moment to look at those numbers again.

You must save over 50 per cent more *per month*, for *40 years*, if you start saving and investing 4 years later than someone who started at 21. If you get started age 40, you can save just 30 per cent of what you would have to put away if you waited another 10 years. Even that jump from age 25 to 35 is a whopping 2.8x increase in the monthly required savings rate.

Does the save-monthly consistently thing feel totally improbable for you? Expect your income or earnings to be up-and-down, or maybe an inheritance or gambling win to come in at some stage? Then let's look at a lump sum scenario . . .

Scenario 2: The lump sum

How big does a single investment have to be to get to that £1,000,000 by 65 metric?

These are the seven examples:[14]

1. Save and invest £11,400 at age 21.
2. Save and invest £18,700 at age 25.
3. Save and invest £30,700 at age 30.
4. Save and invest £50,400 at age 35.
5. Save and invest £83,000 at age 40.
6. Save and invest £224,500 at age 50.
7. Save and invest £608,000 at age 60.

Twenty-one-year-old me is kicking myself right now. For rather than investing my savings from all those night shifts and internships, I kept my money in the bank for several years. Whoops. But no one told me this stuff, even with parents who thought about money as much as mine.

Cutting the same principles another way: at 10 per cent average return per year, anything you have in savings doubles every 7 years. At 9 per cent, it doubles every 8 years. It is hard to overemphasise what a powerful force this is. But this is compounding of returns and exponential growth. It is a J-curve. Almost imperceptible accumulation to start with, that then escalates at stunning speed given more time. *This* is the power of compounding. And the power of having even small amounts of money, sooner.

You may neither care about reaching a seven-figure number nor want to wait until retirement age, or think these numbers are totally irrelevant for you for a host of reasons. **What matters is the reality that small numbers compound up to lottery win amounts in periods of time that seem interminable when you** are 20, but the blink of an eye when you are 40, forget about 50 or 60.

Granted, inflation is going to have reduced some of your purchasing power if we are talking 30 or 40 years. However, not nearly as much as for cash sitting in the bank.

Many of us will fall into both the 'squirrel' or 'lump sum' scenarios at different points in our lives, or unfortunately neither. Having enough financial headroom to save and invest money is not a given, neither is access or the ability to get jobs that enable it.

If, however, you have a chance to earn and save a few hundred extra pounds in the first decade or two of your working life, it matters. If you can tuck something away and save a lump, it matters.

People are out there telling you to 'live your dreams' and 'follow your passion' or find work–life balance. But not many people are out there telling you to optimise for earning or saving an extra £100 per month aged 21 on top of your living expenses. Or doing everything you can to scrape together £30k by 30 years old, then invest it, leave it untouched and never save another penny again. When these are possibilities that may well enable you to live your dreams and have time and security to then follow a different passion next. This can be the difference of having enough money in the bank well before retirement to quit a job you hate, or not take a job because it's not a good fit, or to turn up the dial on a whole range of other priorities when you want and how you want. It is what is often colloquially called 'Fuck You Money' – savings that gives you that extra, meaningful freedom.

If you are currently sitting with your head in your hands, silently chastising yourself for starting too late, I will leave you with this Chinese proverb: 'The best time to plant a tree was 20 years ago. The second-best time is now.'

It is never too late.

It is also never too early.

Luca

The only way I was able to change careers and move countries was because I was thoughtful about money when I was younger, when I worked for a big organisation. I wasn't saving for that, but it gave me the option when I turned out to need it.

I had underestimated how much I would have to think about money while being self-employed: it's one of the few metrics you have for how you are doing when you don't have a boss to tell you 'Well done' or a promotion to get. On top of that, money is reliant on my input, but not necessarily correlated with that input. I can work hard on something new for three months and barely earn anything from it. It can really mess with your head.

This is the first year my business itself has fully covered my living expenses, rather than bits and pieces of old contract work related to my prior career. As this was happening, I realised that my money stress wasn't needing more per se, but needing more predictability. I've just taken on some part-time work for a local university. The regular pay cheque is going make a huge difference on this front.

MONEY INEQUALITY AND THE GENDER PAY GAP

When it comes to earning money, a significant proportion of people are operating in systems where the odds are stacked against them from the start. If you are female. If you are a person of colour. If you are LGBTQIA+. If you are intersectional. This is not politics or opinion. This is statistically and provably true.

I am going to focus on discrimination against women, who are the largest of these groups, but know that this is not because the issues do not exist, at an even larger scale, for the other groups.

Let's start with the gender pay gap. There is not a country in the world that doesn't have one. Data from the World Economic Forum (WEF) shows that the wage gap globally (the ratio of the wage of women to that of men in a similar position) is still approximately 37 per cent and the income gap (the ratio of the total wage and non-wage income of women to that of men) remains close to 51 per cent.[15] Looking at economic participation and opportunity for women overall, the WEF reports that only 58.3 per cent of the gap between women and men globally has been closed. On the current rate of improvement, it would take over *267 years* to close this gap worldwide.

And in case you are optimistically thinking that it's just a few particularly bad laggards dragging down most high performers, then let me rob you of that faith in humanity. The top 5th percentile of countries has a remaining gap to close of about 18 per cent, versus the bottom 5th one of about 60 per cent.[16]

What begin as pay disparities then feed through into pension disparities. Men have substantially more private pension wealth than women, with this gap widening as ages increase. Median pension wealth, i.e. their 'pot' of pension savings, for men aged 65–69 in the UK is just over £212,000. For women in the same age bracket, it is just £35,000. In about half of couples with pensions, one partner has 90 per cent of any pension pot. This links directly to women being more likely to end up in poverty post a divorce or on becoming widowed, especially if they are mothers and divorce after the age of 45.[17]

Moreover, we then have the motherhood penalty. I've thrown a hefty amount of stats at you already in this section, so how about we look at a nice chart?[18]

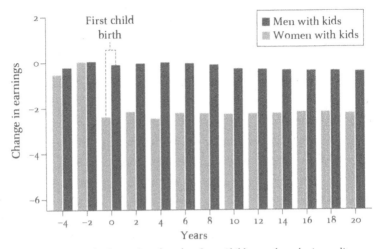

Source: Chart, author's own based on data from *Children and gender inequality: Evidence from Denmark*, National Bureau of Economic Research

This is a chart which shows you that even in one of the most gender-equal countries in the world – one with equal, year-long, paid maternity and paternity leave for parents, one that offers public nursery care for children under three for the equivalent of a few hundred pounds a month (less than half of the average cost in the UK[19]) – Denmark, women's earnings drop significantly after having children. Men's do not.

The authors of this paper find, in fact, that having children creates a gender gap in earnings of around 20 per cent.[20] Not just in the years immediately after the birth, but in the long run. This is the motherhood penalty. Even in egalitarian Denmark.

And this motherhood penalty has been confirmed in study after study, in country after country, time and time again. In the UK, for example, women's employment falls from above 90 per cent to below 75 per cent when they become mothers, with the pay of those who remain in work stagnating and their hours falling from 40 to below 30. In contrast, fathers' employment rate and hours hardly change, and their pay continues to grow.[21]

COVID, of course, exacerbated much of this. Fathers were much less likely than mothers to be laid off in the US during the pandemic, even after controlling for factors such as race, age and education.[22] Not only that, but this 'fatherhood premium' was higher among lower and mid-earning workers.

Even in set-ups where the mother out-earns the father, data shows that female employment falls by at least 13 per cent during the first years of parenthood and remains at this lower level for the next decade.[23] Lower-wage fathers meanwhile stay in paid work at much higher rates and for longer hours. It is women who dial down work and dial up family, and men who do the reverse.

So much of this links and speaks to a profound problem in our societies: the structural undervaluation of caregiving. Yet how many young girls come out of formal education expecting the world to be at their feet? After all, they get better grades in school than the boys (at all ages, and in all subjects. Yep, even STEM).[24] Women get more degrees, both undergraduate and postgraduate, than men.[25,26] They get more graduate jobs than men.[27] All of this suggests that women are not planning to be the ones who step back. They are not working this hard or educating themselves so well to not put their skills to use. But our societies make it incredibly hard to work and be a caregiver. And, eventually, something breaks. And social norms dictate that it breaks for people on one side of the equation more than the other.

No matter how egalitarian your relationship or progressive your industry, it is impossible to outrun this tidal wave entirely. And it is even worse for lower earners. Countless studies from pre-COVID times show that the motherhood penalty in earnings is most severe among lower earning and mid-earning workers. These findings were affirmed further in COVID: mothers did more of the childcare and housework irrespective of their pre-COVID relative pay, and they did much more if paid less than their partners. This from the Institute for Fiscal Studies in the UK: 'Indeed, lower-paid mothers did double the amount of housework and 41 per cent more childcare than higher paid fathers, while higher paid mothers did 6 per cent more house-work and 22 per cent more childcare than lower-paid fathers.'[28]

Let me be crystal clear: this is a call to arms to improve this disgraceful reality for every woman, *especially* those on lower incomes. We can, should and *must* work to change every single part of the incredibly complex equation that means the gender pay gap persists. Many of which we have touched on at various points: political and economic issues such as the availability of childcare, societal issues such as overrepresentation of women in lower paid sectors and roles, and the norms that still make it harder for men to be lead parents. There are many, many books that dive deeper into this topic than I can or could. But the implicit truth this raises is worth spelling out here: that this is an incredibly complex and persistent issue. One which is unlikely to be perfectly resolved in any of our working lives. Which, in turn, should have significant implications when we consider all things money. **Earning well, spending sensibly and investing wisely all matter *more* for women and other marginalised groups.**

So how to practically act on this?

Start by putting at least one money dial on your dashboard: perhaps it is an earnings dial. Or perhaps you have space – mental and monetary – for two: one for earning and one for saving. Perhaps one day there will be ones for investing and donating and a pension as well.

Remember that each and every one of these dials is meant to get adjusted as needs or opportunities arise. Dial your earning level up to max when a well-paid new role presents itself. Tweak the savings dial down a few notches when you are doing the house up that you spent years and years clawing together the

deposit for. But you cannot adjust something you are not explicitly considering.

What matters here is that we each consider money more than
we otherwise would. That if the current societal structures
around money impact us negatively, then we need to consider
money even further.

A way we can ensure we do that is to put money considera-
tions, deliberately and separately, into our dials framework. That
way, we stand a chance of both maximizing the outcomes that
we want, and need, money to enable. And that we have the
stability, access and power to ensure that structural disadvantage, where it exists, becomes a feature of the past rather than
the present or the future.

You will find my favourite books and resources to help you
dive deeper into what this could mean for you on page 227.

Chapter 11

IMPACTFUL WORK

'WORK IS ABOUT a search for daily meaning as well as daily bread, for recognition as well as cash, for astonishment rather than torpor; in short, for a sort of life rather than a Monday through Friday sort of dying.'[1]

An American writer and historian wrote these words back in 1974. Language choice aside (yes, I had to google 'torpor': it is a state of physical or mental inactivity), they feel more relevant than ever.

Contributing to something bigger than oneself is a fundamental part of the human ideal, of the human experience. It matters to the vast majority of us. But it also matters to some more than others.

Women are, by almost every metric, more pro-social than men. They donate more to charity.[2] They are more likely to act as carers to those close to them who are in need.[3] They volunteer more.[4] They vote in elections more, they give blood more than men.[5,6]

Furthermore, women are more likely than men to choose direct people-helping professions like social work, psychology, teaching or nursing.[7] Yes, the ones that tend to be lower paid. Which is why I am going to end this book on an argument to expand how we think about this very topic.

It is not that women should care *or* earn money. It is that women can care in a variety of ways *and* build a resilient and fulfilling life, of which money and many other dials can be a part.

THE POLITICS OF INEVITABILITY

It is a feature of many important ideas that they seem self-evident or natural to the point of invisibility.

A self-evident truth is that any discussion of impact is a discussion about *change*. And that change requires doing things *differently*. That what we want to come next is something different to what is happening today.

Yet, living in a present which is shadowed by 70 or so years of the greatest and fastest social and technological change in any period of human history, it is easy to fall into an assumption that change, well, just happens.

Timothy Snyder, a Yale historian, describes this as 'the politics of inevitability'.[8] That we fall into a trap of believing that the future is simply, inevitably, going to be more of the present. That we know how the world is changing. That there are no alternative versions of the future. So, nothing we do today will change any outcomes.

But, in fact, any particular version of the future is not inevitable – forget about one that many of us crave: one that is better than today.

Just take a second and sit with that. It is simultaneously terrifying, inspiring and daunting.

There is no default path to a more equal, inclusive or just society. We each – all – must *do* the myriad things that will, hopefully, get us there.

We must do the work.

We must bring about the change.

Nadia

I became a primary school teacher because I love working with kids, of course. It is a job that is all about having influence and impact on children's lives. Going through the NQT years are so much harder than they had to be though. I've suggested and implemented some policies in my school to make it better for those coming behind me. I have so many more ideas and am now discussing them both with my union representative and my academy trust. We can and should do this all better. It shouldn't be this hard.

HOW TO MAKE A CHANGE

In a world which is as complex and layered as ours, it is vanishingly rare to have a straight line from action to impact. There are normally a bunch of contributing factors, and people, and lucky breaks, which help bring about change, especially on a national level. Gina Martin is one of the few who has managed a much more direct route.

In the summer of 2017, Martin went to an open-air concert in central London. She rebuffed a man who had been verbally harassing her, and his response was to take a photo underneath her skirt – so-called 'upskirting'.

Remarkably, Martin saw the photo and managed to grab the perpetrator's phone. She then got away from his attempt to physically restrain her, and ran, evidence in hand, to the event security zone and then to the police to report what had happened. The furious man was chasing her every step of the way, seemingly in no doubt that the greater crime here had been a woman who had belittled him in front of his friends and relieved him of what was at that point a weapon for sexual assault.

As they comforted her, the police informed Martin that no crime had been committed. All they could or would do is ensure the photo was deleted. They then considered the case closed.

And thus began Martin's campaign to make upskirting illegal. A feat she succeeded at less than two years later.[9]

Very few of us take awful experiences in our lives and vow to address them at a macro level. Forget about having the tenacity and wherewithal to reach such a far-ranging and impactful conclusion. This is an incredibly inspiring example of activism creating impact.

Yet activism is not the only way of bringing about change. It is not even a primary option in many cases; if only making more things illegal offered the protections and opportunities that so many of us hope to see more of in the future.

Whatever change we want to engender, we need to have a theory of how that change is going to come about.

Let's take a moment to contemplate:

- How does a system get changed?
- How does an organisation get changed?
- How does a person's opinion and actions get changed?

These are, frankly, enormous questions. Ones that many an academic, countless books and infinite activists' chats have tried to answer. People can, and do, spend their entire lives trying to find the answers, both in theory and in practice. I spent a not-insignificant amount of time reading up on all of this, with the goal of distilling something consumable, and ultimately actionable, here. That list looked something like this: changing social norms, starting social cascades, a discussion about how public and private institutions influence individuals, how laws are set and public policies made, how access to resources matters, who the stakeholders are and where the power lies. I quickly realised this very approach would be part of the problem.

The 'how' does not have to be all-encompassing. It does not have to be approved by academics or objectively perfect in every way. You do not need to be a full-time activist or know how to get the law changed, or even want to. There are rarely quick solutions for hard problems. Let me say that again: **there are rarely quick solutions for hard problems.** There are a million dimensions to a better, fairer world. Huge numbers of levers with little leverage, collectively pulled, make for big change. The biggest or 'best' one might not be the one that is available to you, right here, right now, or even further down your unique life path. But there will absolutely be one, or several, on that journey.

We need everyone to have an impact dial and feel empowered to use it. Individual choices plus collective action plus structural accountability drive systemic change. No single person is going to be able to move every part of this equation, or even one piece entirely.

My theory of change is 'all and', not 'either or'. We need people on *all* the paths to make change happen. We need policymakers' actions, academics' insights and activists' hustle. We need the kick-ass CEOs, and the inclusive line managers, and the new hires brave enough to point out that something isn't right about how things have always been done. We need the political parties, and big corporates that employ millions, and the entrepreneurs, and the nurses and doctors, and the public servants of all stripes. We need the people who care in *all* the places.

I have had countless conversations with those both ahead of and behind me on various career paths. Almost without exception, those conversations with women have included time on the topic of impact. The consistent undertones of so many of these heart-to-hearts are guilt and fear: guilt that we aren't doing enough; fear that we aren't contributing sufficiently. This is, I think, a very *female* reaction function: we have been raised in a world that has us believe that our value is in no small part related to how much care we provide to others.

I absolutely grapple with these questions myself. Am I being selfish by pursuing a career that is not primarily based on helping people? Am I tinkering at the edges with regards to the causes I care about because they are not at the heart of my day-to-day? Am I donating enough? Am *I* enough?

But two things can be true.

One: that if we set the bar so high that the only threshold is total dedication to 'the cause', whatever that may be, then we are closing off a million potential routes to change and spurning a million people who could action it. Which is a disaster, both for the outcomes we seek and for our own personal fulfilment and meaning.

But more than that, we are also actively shaking out the very people who are most likely to bring about the most change in the places that most need it. The ones who deeply care and the ones who hold themselves to a standard of real action are the ones who are going to feel most adrift in places where caring and change are not a core purpose. And they are the ones who are most susceptible to the message that it must be all, or nothing. These are the *very* people we need, and we need them to be where change is hardest. That is where the work needs to be done most. Because that is precisely where we need *more*; of them, and of the caring they provide. Those who care can not, *must not*, abandon the field to those who think this work does not need to be done. To those who do not care.

The second truth is that the threshold is also higher for some of us. When you reach, or are on a path to, a comfortable life, it is natural to expect more of yourself. And so you – and I – should. To whom much is given, much will be required, the oft-quoted Bible verse tells us. The way 'impact' expresses itself on my dials should absolutely be different now that I have achieved a level of financial security or career security or the like.

Do you already have an obvious area in your life that is geared towards making an impact? It might be your work or some volunteering that you already do. The work a teacher does is inherently impactful, but there are aspects to a teacher's work that are decidedly 'about' that impact on children, and aspects that are about the income, or the intellectual rigour. Your dials can be a helpful way of peeling apart these different aspects of a part of your life, and prioritising them accordingly when opportunities or needs arise (and indeed, fall away). Looking back to Chapter 3 where you identified your dials, this is where getting the right level of detail can really help.

The level at which your impact dial(s) are set is also going to be reflective of the season of life you are in. You might be in a stage of life which helps, or hinders, where your impact dial can be set, but thinking consciously about this can help you be at peace with this current reality or make some changes that enable you to get those dials to where you truly want them to be. When you have more or less seniority at work; or more or less time available for other things; or control over the schedule of your days; or when your family and friends need you more, or indeed less.

Questions to ask yourself

- Is there a topic or area of the world in which you want to effect change?
- What could an impact dial represent to you?
- What does 'making a difference' feel and look like for you?

_____

_____

_____

_____

Emelia

I run my own small business and recently got invited to a roundtable event with my local MP and a group of other small business owners and entrepreneurs. I never would have gone to something like that before, but I spoke up about childcare, and about parental leave, and financial support for the self-employed. Everyone looked at me like I had three heads. Not a single other person around the table spoke up to agree with me. I was so shocked because I know some of them and we have talked about it before. It has made me even more determined to keep speaking up about these things.

It's not my day job, it is not what my business is about, but I barely held my business together when my daughter was born, and now nursery is crushingly expensive. I am going to keep talking about this wherever I can because I think it stops so many people from making the leap to work for themselves, or means they can't do what they want to do either as parents or as business owners because they are physically, mentally and financially stretched to break-ing point.

MAKING AN IMPACT EFFECTIVELY

Keeping our theory of change broad means we can include as many people as possible in the project of maximising impact. However, there are some lessons we can learn from those who have already done significant in-depth work on the 'how's and 'where's of making an impact, and indeed maximising that impact. Especially when we want to get practical about what all this means in our lives and how we could or should express it in a Dials framework.

The Effective Altruism (EA) project is 'a research field and practical community that aims to find the best ways to help others, and put them into practice'.[10] Formalised by a group of scholars at the University of Oxford a decade or so ago, what is especially compelling about EA as an approach is that it is not calling for a particular solution to the world's problems, but a way of thinking – one that encourages people to think critically about their available resources, skills and choices, and then assess the best ways to make the most effective difference. The founders argue that **we can all apply EA no matter how much we want to focus on doing good, and in any area of our lives**. They say that what matters, irrespective of how much we want to contribute, is that 1) we try to make those efforts as effective as possible and 2) we use the following values to underpin our approach to helping others:[11]

- Prioritisation: finding the best ways to help rather than just working to make any difference at all.
- Impartial altruism: all people count equally, so focus on the most neglected groups and those who don't have as much power to protect their own interests.
- Open truth-seeking: considering many different ways to help

and seeking to find the best ones, being constantly open and curious, and ready to change one's views.

- Collaborative spirit: we can achieve more if we work together.

EA is not about finding a magic bullet, or ignoring all other priorities, or committing ourselves entirely to 'the cause'. It is about understanding where and how we each can take achievable steps which deliver tangible results. For some, that will be by joining the EA research community, but for most it will be through using the output of that research to make a practical difference. Through our work or how we use our money.

I share it here not because it is perfect, or indeed the only way of thinking about impact. However, you can use the work already done here as a guide to help you find a way to add an impact dimension to an existing dial or group of dials on your dashboard.

Through work

We have already spent much of the book talking about how work can facilitate our lives. **Work can also facilitate the impact we want to have on the world.**

If you start working full-time aged 21, retire aged 65, take eight weeks of holiday (including bank holidays) a year, two lots of 6-month parental leave and another couple of 6-month breaks, you are going to clock up somewhere in the region of 70,000–100,000 hours of work, the range being dictated by 8- to 12-hour workdays.

This is an extraordinary amount of output into the world. If it takes 10,000 hours of practice to become an expert, many of us could do that many times over.[12]

For some, this will be by taking a job directly in a field which addresses some of the more pressing global problems, be that at the start or middle or end of a 40+-year working life. Or starting a business or organisation that does the same – again, the time horizons for this are long. Or by finding ways to use their existing skills to contribute to these problems by volunteering or advocating, or getting access to or an understanding of powerful organisations, public and private, which set policy and influence people's behaviours and choices.

EA advocates strongly for finding the work that fits us better so that we can maximise our possible leverage. That leverage being the money, attention, skill, reputations and network we are each able to mobilise, knowing that these are all likely to take decades to build to their peak. This, again, ties strongly into much of what we have already discussed on the topics of work and career fulfilment – how we each can flourish so that we can do our best work, be our best selves and then make the maximum positive impact possible. Being clear about your dashboard, having the right dials on top and being able to adjust the levels on them is a method for doing this. After all, much of the change we desire is more likely to arise if we can find a way to thrive in the current status quo. Because change takes energy. And time. And patience. And resilience.

The words of Nobel prize-winning author Toni Morrison are a guiding light on how to have impact with our work: 'When you get these jobs that you have been so brilliantly trained for, just remember that your real job is that if you are free, you need to free somebody else. If you have some power, then your job is to empower somebody else. This is not just a grab-bag candy game.'[13]

Amelie

I will only work for clients who have a strong social impact. I build technology solutions so what I do can be very valu-

able, and not many charities can afford it elsewhere. At one stage I took part in a VC accelerator, but I found it incredibly demotivating. I love that the clients I support have a mission. It is the filter through which I see, and decide, everything when it comes to my career.

Through money

Money matters – in our dials and as part of EA. Donating effectively, to the most effective charities, is a core part of how many of us can make a difference. This, according to the tenets of EA, comprises the following:

- Identify a promising cause to support: by assessing causes across their importance (how much good could arise from working on a specific problem), their tractability (how solvable the problem is) and neglectedness (how overlooked it is in terms of committed resources), EA researchers have rigorously demonstrated that some causes, charities, organisations or actions can help 100 times as many people when given the same amount of resource.[14,15]
- Choose an excellent organisation working to support the cause: those that rely on evidence, have high cost-effectiveness and transparency, and a strong track record. Organisations such as GiveWell (givewell.org), Giving What We Can (givingwhatwecan.org) and Effective Altruism Funds (funds.effectivealtruism.org) collate much of the research, provide easy places to donate and pledge to give on an ongoing basis.
- Pick an efficient way to donate: using corporate donation-matching by your employer is a low-lift way of doubling your donations: 65 per cent of the Fortune 500 companies in the US offer matching gift programmes for example.[16] Using salary

211

sacrifice schemes, registering for Gift Aid in the UK or making a tax-deductible charitable donation in the US are all ways you can make an equivalent dollar or pound go further.

A particularly powerful piece of consciously thinking about donating in this way is that it sets an intention. We discussed earlier in the book how your dashboard can be a wonderful commitment device. So too can a dial. And what better commitment than a donating dial?

Questions to ask yourself

- How can you make more impact via your existing work?
- Do you want to change your work to be more directly related to impact?
- Do you have an impact dial which sits alongside your work, or a volunteering dial or the like?
- Can your money dial in fact be a money group: a dial for earning, a dial for donating and a dial for investing and saving?

_____

_____

_____

_____

Nic

I donate 10 per cent of my after-tax income every year. I have different direct debits set up, so it is all automatic. One day, I will move that to pre-tax, but for now it's what I can manage without having to think too much about it. That would be the dial adjustment I would – will – make when I can.

THE IMPACT OF ONE AMAZING PERSON

While the lessons of the EA movement are instructive, there is a smaller scale to consider before we end – **the vast impact a single person can have on an other.** If you have no financial room to donate right now, if you can't re-track a career at this point in your life, or effect change in an organisation of which you are a part, or frankly, if your dials are just turned up to other things in this season of your life, the impact you can have on someone else is still enormous.

> **Asha**
>
> *Faith is my source, my perspective. It has to be a huge piece of my dashboard. Being able to share that to make it more tangible to others is really important to me. That comes out in a few ways in my life – so a little grouping of three dials. I attend a community Bible group every two weeks. It's nearby and I find it's a much better fit for me than going to church, which I used to do when I was younger but haven't for, gosh, many years now. I host a prayer group every Friday morning. This is on Zoom and I make time for it no matter what else is going on in my life – time zone changes, family stuff, work – everything centres around those 30 minutes. I'm also writing a series of devotionals and reflection journals as guides for people to delve into and reflect on key themes and Bible verses. It's my contribution to my community, something I think about a lot in relation to both my faith and my purpose.*

When I think of one person who has had a massively outsized positive impact on my life, I think of Lora.

I was in my late twenties, out of The Progressively Less Shit Years (see page 106) at work, getting objectively good at my job, at last. I was operating most days in a flow state, ticking the psychological need boxes of autonomy, competence and relatedness. However, it slowly began to dawn on me that what had got me 'here' would not get me 'there'. 'There' being the next rung on the ladder.

The things that got people 'there' were not the things I was excellent at, and it became increasingly clear that I needed to be excellent to excel – both from a progression and fulfilment point of view. I didn't know or see what that role could be, and fell into a funk as I panicked about not knowing how to create a change, or even what I should be changing to.

Thankfully Lora, the wonderful female partner who ran the business unit I sat in, noticed my malaise. She took it upon herself to get me, incredibly reluctantly and only after I had secured another (frankly, bad) job offer, to talk to her about what was going on. She helped me do some serious introspection about my skills and strengths, and this, combined with her knowledge of the firm and her personal sponsorship, helped me get into a role where I could truly thrive.

It is not an understatement to say that Lora changed my life. Getting into that new seat set up my dials of work and career and money in ways I couldn't have imagined. In turn, that enabled me to do, and enjoy rather than just survive through, so many of the things that define my life: motherhood, writing and, yes, more career and more work and more personal fulfilment, as well as more time, space and resources for impact.

I am sure most of us have a story of a person who took a moment, or several, to stop and help us along the way. And we should not underestimate the potential that these acts of kindness, be they big or small, have throughout a lifetime.

Journalist Ezra Klein encourages us to think of ourselves not as solely an individual but 'as a node for social, political and moral contagion'.[17] He argues that individual attitudes collectively add up to social attitudes, and then to social and political change, describing that 'oftentimes the way politics changes is that enough individuals have changed'. There are grand examples of this; one Klein flags is how attitudes to civil rights have changed over the past 100 or so years in countries such as the US and the UK. But there are much more personal ones too: he describes 'catching' veganism from his wife, and how he in turn has passed it on to others around him.

This is an incredibly powerful way of framing how we can each have impact in the world. We are each a point, a node, in a network of humans that makes up the entire world. **We absolutely have the power to influence those closest to us, which then links to the next person, and the next and the next.** So much of the influencing that is getting done in the world is not happening from the bully pulpit of high political office or a TV screen or words in books or scrolling through social media. It is from those whose skin we can touch, whose words we feel as they are spoken to us. It is those we have grown up with, or away from, or spend time with. We have opportunities every day to set the tone – in our workplaces, in our families, in our communities, on our travels and in our neighbourhoods.

Marc

Impact is a dashboard value that is not currently expressed in my life. I'm interested in how small communities can be built – how they self-sustain and how they help people thrive. I'm not able to make it my work so I haven't done anything with it, even though I read so much about examples around the world and have a few ideas zapping

> *around my head. I wonder if I can reframe it, think about*
> *something smaller – perhaps having it as a dial where I*
> *impact a handful of people around me.*

Reminding ourselves of the impact we can have on those imme-diately around us is important. In a work context, we do not have to wait to be CEO (a level most of us will not be able to or want to reach) to make a difference or have impact. Treating people well matters. Hiring more fairly, mentoring (traditional and reverse), sponsoring, suggesting and implementing policy changes, directing business to marginalised groups and ethical businesses. Speaking up in rooms full of people who don't have your life experience. All of these things can have a meaningful impact. Yes, a little more seniority will help on many of these fronts, but it is neither a necessary nor sufficient condition for impact.

It will come as no surprise if you have made it this far through the book that I care deeply about ending discrimina-tion against women and enabling more people to live happy, fruitful work and personal lives, especially while parenting. So, while the tenets of EA have absolutely shaped my thoughts on which charities I donate to, and indeed how much I can and should be donating, I am still, always, going to be seizing every opportunity to make a difference on this front too. Indeed, I think about these as separate dials: I have a donating dial that sits in a money grouping and, for lack of a better way of describ-ing it, a feminism dial which sits alongside my work and career dials. Because it is intimately linked to the impact I can have in the male-dominated spaces in which I operate.

My feminism dial has got me into a fair few sticky situations over the years. I cannot help but take an opportunity to have awkward, for the other participants at least, conversations about the gender pay gap or the motherhood penalty or the still heavily male make-up of leadership in my industry. I might not always find the most graceful way through, but every now and again the matrix glitches enough to make me think that it is not all for nothing.

Of course, there are many examples where I didn't speak up or didn't have the most effective plan to bring about change. It is not that I have this dial perfectly worked out, or indeed that it is always turned up to the max. But I am consciously trying and learning, and working to make effective use of the fact that I am a decidedly not shy woman working in a company, and in an industry, that many others look to. Change is catching. And we are each a node for contagion.

It can be easy to get lost in the big picture. To expect that anything less than explicitly and obviously fixing massive problems in the world is a failure.

But it is not.

The ways we can each have impact are potentially limitless. Explicitly adding a dial or two which speaks to the practical actions we can take – which themselves, by definition, will be limited – is a way to ensure it actually happens.

> *Questions to ask yourself*
> - What are the people, or things, or places, or events you care deeply about?
> - How can you express this care in your dials?
> - What platform do you have, what skills do you possess, what energy can you contribute that could have an impact?
>
> _____
> _____
> _____
> _____

There are ways some of us can express this directly in our work – like a nurse in the day-to-day of what he does, saving lives and caring for people. Or it might be more personal than that. If you care about climate change, perhaps you are making changes about what you eat, or how you travel, or what you consume. If you care about better representation, maybe you factor that into who you vote for, or hire, or mentor.

Let me share one final quote: 'If we remember those times and places – and there are so many – where people have behaved magnificently, this gives us the energy to act, and at least the possibility of sending this spinning top of a world in a different direction.'[18]

Those words were written by Howard Zinn, a historian, philosopher and World War II veteran. Zinn had seen and thought about so much of the worst that humans have to offer each other. And yet he encouraged us to be hopeful about change. He reminds us that there is not one cataclysmic moment that will bring about a better society, but we will 'zig-zag' our way there based on small acts multiplied by millions of people.

We are those people.

You and me.

We can do small acts, and big ones, that bring about a better world.

And we can do more of them, better, if we use mental models and decision frameworks that allow us to live, to work *and* to thrive. Right here. Right now. In this world as it is. Because that is how we create the future we want to see.

CONCLUSION

I DIDN'T WRITE this book to persuade you that banking is *the* answer to tricky questions about career paths or life choices, as much as it has been a wonderful choice for me.

I wrote it because there are many, *many* ways to live a fulfilling life. But almost all of them are going to be made harder, and more prone to combustion and burnout and disappointment, if we use the toxic mental model of work–life balance as our guide along the way.

Instead, I've offered you the framework of The Dials. With its four simple, but meaningful, components: dashboard, dials, levels and resilience. A framework which enables you to stay true to what is important to you in your life. A reflection of who you are and what matters to you. A mental model that speaks to the kind of life you want to live and what you want to achieve with it, and that is inherently dynamic – just as life, needs and opportunities are.

It starts with your life goals, your values, your priorities: the things that make you uniquely you and speak to how you want to live your precious time on this earth. This is your dashboard. This is the foundation on top of which everything else sits.

The dials come next. These are the component parts of a rich, varied and fulfilling life. Ones that allow you to express your dashboard in the real world. Over the long term. And to thrive in your life, today. Not a conflict-prone duality of work and life; because 'work' isn't one unique thing. It could be the dial of your current job and the adjacent but distinct dials of the promotion you are working towards, or the new job you are searching for.

'Life' isn't one homogenous bucket either. It is friendships. It is lovers. It is kids. It is travel, or fitness, or rest. It is money. It is a house move or a wedding. Or donating to charity, or building a meditation practice, or sponsoring a group of young people in your field. It is learning. It is your significant other. It is your relationship with yourself and the things you need, yes need, to do to honour that. Each is a dial. Dials will come on and off your dashboard as life changes, but you will always have a set of dials that reflect the component parts of life.

Dials are dynamic by design. The levels on your dials are meant to be changed. Opportunities reveal themselves, needs press down on us, life happens. Things in our lives get dialled up or dialled down accordingly as capacity and seasons of life change. Sometimes the reality of a situation requires you to be more dedicated to one or two areas of your life. Sometimes you can run several priorities together. Sometimes this is in our control, sometimes it's not. But intensity should not, cannot, be fixed. The levels on your dials can, will and should consciously change.

And lastly, this framework reminds you that you cannot, should not, expect to do this wild and precious thing called life without support. Instead, we should take opportunities to build in resilience to our plans, our bodies and our lives wherever and whenever we can. By optimising our dashboard values and goals to find them in many versions of the future and understanding the reasons behind – the why – of what we want. By adding dials that allow us to stay in the game, healthy and calm and strong, for as long as possible. By assessing choices, not only by their dream outcome, but also by whether they will allow us to adjust the levels on our dials when we may need to.

SHIFTING YOUR DIALS

Baking or banking . . . That was the decision Alexina was weighing up when we left her back in Chapter 2 (page 30). If you possess about as much patience as I do, you will have already googled Alexina and *MasterChef* and discovered that, yes, Alexina is a real person. A real person who made it to the final of *MasterChef*, is now a cookbook author and is excelling in her professional food career.

Alexina started her working life thinking that her dashboard was about financial stability and proving her independence. She wanted to show her family, who had fought so hard to get themselves to where they were – and her to the University of Cambridge – that she would not be a burden. Guiding lights which led her to nearly seven years in banking and consulting. Years through which she developed her passion for all things food, rather than the trading floor; years that gave her a depth of experience which empowered her to decide what was right for her, and to ultimately close the door on what was not; years in which she gained the knowledge that cooking, and the connection it brings to both people and to place, was more important, more foundational and more authentic to her and how she wanted to live her life than anything else.

She now has a very different group of dials on her dashboard that represent 'career': a 'supper club' dial, a 'cookbook writing' dial and a 'TV cooking show' dial – dials which are currently turned all the way up. As she describes it, she has a 'window of opportunity' in the world of cooking, and she needs to throw herself into it right now. This is the season of life she is in.

Alexina explained to me how she cultivates her dashboard value of connection through each of these dials: having her friends act as servers during her supper clubs because she is so pressed for time to see them any other way in this season of her life; how asking for their help, showing her needs and allowing them to support her and experience her passions alongside her has brought them closer than ever; how researching her books and recipes has led her to so many new people and their homes and kitchens, to share food, and culture, and flavours, and histories.

She also explained how some other dials – like finding a partner – in her life were set to low right now, but how she knew it wouldn't be forever. How she wouldn't be getting done what she is doing without allowing the people who love her to help, and without ruthlessly prioritising her health. This is what resilience looks like for Alexina right now: asking for help and having her health dial as the one that is always on the highest setting.

I share Alexina's story not because we all need some massive quarter-life, or mid-life, or indeed retirement-age, reset or change of direction. I share it because it can take time to discover the values, priorities and goals that, if we can see them clearly, will help be the foundation of a fulfilled and successful life. I share her story because these things can, and do, change. We all come from hugely different backgrounds, and have hugely different dreams and expectations for our lives, as well as opportunities and challenges in front of us.

Specifying your dashboard, creating your dials, setting your levels and thinking about how you are factoring resilience into it all is about finding a better way to express – out loud and to ourselves – what we all spend so much time talking and thinking about: living and working, together, in all its complex, intertwined, messy glory. It is about moving from a two-dimensional concept to a four-dimensional one.

This is about finding a personal, intentional and dynamic way of thinking about your life so you can actually live it. When times are easy. When times are hard. And everything in between.

So first, create those dials. *Your* dials.

Then get shifting them. No more one-size-fits-all. No more balance. No more binary.

Your dashboard. *Your* dials. *Your* levels. All as resilient as they can be.

A DIALABLE LIFE

If we think about our values, our priorities, our goals in life . . .

If we express them thoughtfully through the multiple component parts that make up a rich and varied life: work, career, relationships, health, fitness, creativity, rest, learning, travel, nature, impact, money and so much more . . .

If we consciously and deliberately adjust the intensity with which we are spending our time and energy on those component parts based on the season of life we are in and the opportunities or needs in front of us . . .

If we are honest with ourselves, and each other, about the very real trades that some of this will entail . . .

If we let go of beliefs that passions are found, or that the starting years of our careers are going to be smooth sailing, or that work should be one singular thing that will provide everything that is special and meaningful to us . . .

If we consciously think about money as an independent factor in our lives . . .

If we embrace a theory of change which is 'all and' when it comes to impact, as well as thinking about how we can make the most effective use of our available resources to bring a version of the future that is better than today . . .

If we deeply acknowledge that we cannot, should not, do any of this alone. That it is not only wise to build resilience into our lives, but, when we do, we give ourselves the very best chance of making the very best out of what we have . . .

We can shift our dials and find success in all aspects of ourselves and how we move through the world, instead of trying and failing to find balance between the false binary of life and work. We can live a dialable life.

What a victory that would be.

And what further victories we could all bring about as a result.

MONEY MATTERS
RESOURCES

The Simple Path to Wealth by J. L. Collins (CreateSpace Independent Publishing Platform, 2016)
J. L. Collins is one of the founding voices of the so-called 'financial independence' movement. I recommend this book over many of the others because of its quiet, grounded logic and numerous worked-through examples. It is not the bombastic, celebrity-front-cover version of so many other books in this genre, and is all the better for it. It is very much written for an American audience, but the principles and many of the implementations are applicable for those living all over the world.

The Monevator (monevator.com/) and The Escape Artist (theescapeartist.me) blogs
To counter the US lens of my first recommendation, these blogs are the places to go.
   The Monevator is a personal blog about money, as the authors describe it, 'making, saving, growing and sometimes even spending it'. If I ever have a question about money technicalities (taxes, investing accounts and platforms, tracker funds, mortgages, etc.), this is where I go first. They are not selling anything and share

their own (different) views on investing too, all with the goal of helping you find your own. This is a strong recommend.

The Escape Artist is a more numerous and punchy affair. Start with the 'Start Here' posts to see whether you vibe with it. Even if you don't, the lessons are clear, direct and invaluable. The author is selling resources and coaching, which I cannot vouch for, but the multitude of free resources (including downloadable spreadsheets) is excellent.

Financial Wellness & How to Find It by **Melanie Eusebe (Orion Spring, 2022)**
This book is written by a woman, for women, with countless snippets of real women's stories, challenges and solutions on all things money and financial wellness. This is especially for those who love a worksheet-based book. Practical, useful and impactful.

Money Lessons: How to manage your finances to get the life you want by **Lisa Conway-Hughes (Penguin Life, 2019)**
More super practical and useable advice. This book covers the 'small' stuff (funding a big trip or budgeting a wedding) and the 'big' stuff (mortgages, getting out of debt, retirement), and helps to make money work for you and your life.

Richer, Wiser, Happier: How the world's greatest investors win in markets and life by **William Green (Profile Books, 2022)**
This is very much *not* a book for those looking for copy and paste investing strategies, but if you like people, their stories and the lessons different lives can teach us, all with a markets and investing twist, this is a fantastic read. One which will reinforce the truth that active investing is incredibly difficult, and even the pros get it wrong, but that there is much for us all to learn from their failures and successes along the way.

ACKNOWLEDGEMENTS

I'm not sure 'acknowledgement' is sufficient recognition of the first person on this list, but here it goes anyway . . . Nick: husband, best friend, eye-candy, cheerleader, sounding board, editor, fact-checker, reference-gatherer, responder to children in the dead of night (and all the other hours of the day). You truly do it all and none of this would be here without it, without you. You've not-so-jokingly called this book 'The Philosophy of Rebecca'. If that is true, then it is only one that exists because of the love and patience and fun you have poured into me over the past two decades. I love you. I am infinitely grateful for everything you do, for me and for our boys. And I agree, reluctantly, that not writing this dedication while I was grumpy was a good decision.

To my trio of bests, for you are the very best: Nicole, Emily and Amy. You've always been there for me in more ways than I can count. You all, each, mean the world to me.

I owe a massive debt of gratitude to my agent Rachel Mills. Rachel, you never fail to make time for me, give unbelievably thoughtful, incisive and actionable feedback and advice. And just make stuff happen I couldn't have dreamed of. I'm so lucky to be in your crew.

Next, a huge appreciation to Julia Kellaway. When I got to the stage of book-writing that you swooped in at, I googled the term 'copy editor' as I had no idea how it all worked. I can say now that Google has no idea either, as the results woefully undersell the magic you work. You got the worst of my deadline-missing, imposter-syndrome-suffering, crisis-of-confidence-panicking self and still managed to make this book better than I could have hoped for.

Thank you to the wonderful team at Yellow Kite: for trusting me to make what seemed like a pivot to everyone else but felt so right for me. Especially to Lauren Whelan for believing in me from the start and doing it while being a living, breathing example of living a dialable life. And to Holly Whitaker and Liv Nightingall for so wonderfully guiding me along the way.

Last but by no means least, the broadest and biggest thank you to every single person who graced me with their time, their honesty, their stories, their advice, their support, their feedback, their questions, their disagreements and, most of all, their energy in many, many conversations about all things career, life and love as I worked on this book – and, frankly, in the many years before when it was not even a whisper of an idea. It's a cliché to say this wouldn't be here without you all, but, in this case, it is quite literally true. Thank you. Thank you.

ENDNOTES

INTRODUCTION

1 McKinsey Global Institute, 15 Jul. 2020. COVID-19 and gender equality: Countering the regressive effects. Retrieved from https://www.mckinsey.com/featured-insights/future-of-work/covid-19-and-gender-equality-countering-the-regressive-effects.

2 Andrew, A., Cattan, S., Dias, M. C., Farquharson, C., Kraftman, L., Krutikova, S., Phimister, A. and Sevilla, A., 27 May 2020. Parents, especially mothers, paying heavy price for lockdown. Institute for Fiscal Studies. Retrieved from https://ifs.org.uk/news/parents-especially-mothers-paying-heavy-price-lockdown.

3 Gingerbread, Sep. 2019. Single parents: Facts and figures. Retrieved from https://www.gingerbread.org.uk/what-we-do/media-centre/single-parents-facts-figures/.

4 House of Commons Women and Equalities Committee, 8 Dec. 2020. Unequal impact? Coronavirus and BAME people. Retrieved from https://committees.parliament.uk/publications/3965/documents/39887/default/.

5 Sawo, M., 21 Dec. 2021. An economic recovery for whom? Economic Policy Institute. Retrieved from https://www.epi.org/blog/an-economic-recovery-for-whom-black-womens-employment-gaps-show-important-differences-in-recovery-rates/.

6 Department for Business, Energy & Industrial Strategy, 7 Oct. 2021. Business population estimates for the UK and the regions 2021. Retrieved from https://assets.publishing.service.gov.uk/government/uploads/system/uploads/attachment_data/file/1019907/2021_Business_Population_Estimates_for_the_UK_and_regions_Statistical_Release.pdf.

7 Lacarte, V. and Hayes, J., 5 Nov. 2019. Women's median earnings as a percent of men's, 1985–2018 (full-time, year-round workers) with projections for pay equity, by race/ethnicity. Institute for Women's Policy Research. Retrieved from http://referenceiwpr.wpengine.com/publications/pay-equity-projection-race-ethnicity-2019/.

CHAPTER 1: THE ALTERNATIVE TO WORK–LIFE BALANCE

1 Livingston, G., 8 Jan. 2018. Most dads say they spend too little time with their children; about a quarter live apart from them. Pew Research Center. Retrieved from https://www.pewresearch.org/fact-tank/2018/01/08/most-dads-say-they-spend-too-little-time-with-their-children-about-a-quarter-live-apart-from-them/.

2 Lee, E. and Brown, B., 21 Oct. 2014. Jennifer Garner: No one asks Ben about work–family balance. *Today.* Retrieved from https://www.today.com/popculture/jennifer-garner-no-one-asks-ben-about-work-family-balance-1d80232707.

3 YouGov, 2021. YouGov/RSA survey results. Retrieved from https://docs.cdn.yougov.com/cpcofn1w94/RSA_Key_Workers_210315_1600_W.xls.pdf.

4 YouGov, 2020. YouGov/QMUL survey results. Retrieved from https://docs.cdn.yougov.com/rgskqbhi20/QMULResults_201119_WorkingfromHome_W.pdf.

5 Sapranaviciute-Zabazlajeva, L., Luksiene, D., Virviciute, D., Bobak, M. and Tamosiunas, A., 2017. Link between healthy lifestyle and psychological well-being in Lithuanian adults aged 45–72: A cross-sectional study. *BMJ Open, 7*(4), p. e014240.

6 Steptoe, A., O'Donnell, K., Marmot, M. and Wardle, J., 2008. Positive affect, psychological well-being, and good sleep. *Journal of Psychosomatic Research, 64*(4), pp. 409–15.

7 Solomon, A., 28 Oct. 2021. There's no such thing as 'balancing work and family' . . . Instagram. Retrieved from https://www.instagram.com/p/CVjkhUoM_wa/.

8 Zagefka, H., Houston, D., Duff, L. and Moftizadeh, N., 2021. Combining motherhood and work: effects of dual identity and identity conflict on well-being. *Journal of Child and Family Studies, 30*(10), pp. 2452–60.

CHAPTER 2: YOUR DASHBOARD

1 Locke, E. A. and Latham, G. P., Apr. 1991. A theory of goal setting & task performance. *The Academy of Management Review, 16*(2).

2 Sevdalis, N. and Harvey, N., 2006. Predicting preferences: A neglected aspect of shared decision-making. *Health Expectations*, 9(3), pp. 245–51.

3 Bauckham, G., Lambert, R., Atance, C. M., Davidson, P. S., Taler, V. and Renoult, L., 2019. Predicting our own and others' future preferences: The role of social distance. *Quarterly Journal of Experimental Psychology*, 72(3), pp. 634–42.

4 Beaton, C., 2 Nov. 2017. Humans are bad at predicting futures that don't benefit them. *The Atlantic*. Retrieved from https://www.theatlantic.com/science/archive/2017/11/humans-are-bad-at-predicting-futures-that-dont-benefit-them/544709/.

5 Schroeder, A., 2009. *The Snowball: Warren Buffett and the Business of Life*. Bloomsbury Publishing.

6 Stanford Encyclopedia of Philosophy, 2 Jul. 2022. Aristotle's ethics. Retrieved from https://plato.stanford.edu/entries/aristotle-ethics/.

7 Castro, 11 Sep. 2021. 44. Edward Glaeser Explains why some cities thrive while others fade away [podcast]. Retrieved from https://castro.fm/episode/sXr45i.

8 McIntyre, H., 18 May 2021. Taylor Swift's re-recordings could make her one of the most successful acts in Billboard 200 history. *Forbes*. Retrieved from https://www.forbes.com/sites/hughmcintyre/2021/05/18/taylor-swifts-re-recordings-could-make-her-one-of-the-most-successful-acts-in-billboard-200-history/.

9 Willman, C., 5 Feb. 2008. Taylor Swift's road to fame. *Entertainment Weekly*. Retrieved from https://ew.com/article/2008/02/05/taylor-swifts-road-fame/.

10 Rogers, A., 7 Mar. 2014. Q&A: Why Taylor Swift thinks Nashville is the best place on earth. *Time*. Retrieved from https://time.com/14933/taylor-swift-nashville-interview/.

11 The Knowledge Project, n.d. Ryan Holiday: A stoic life [podcast, episode 128]. Retrieved from https://fs.blog/knowledge-podcast/ryan-holiday-2/.

CHAPTER 3: YOUR DIALS

1 Silver, L., Van Kessel, P., Huang, C., Clancy, L. and Gubbala, S., 18 Nov. 2021. What makes life meaningful? Views from 17 advanced economies. Pew Research Center. Retrieved from https://www.pewresearch.org/global/2021/11/18/what-makes-life-meaningful-views-from-17-advanced-economies/.

2 Kierkegaard, S., 2015. *The Diary of Søren Kierkegaard*. Citadel Press, edited by P. Rohde.

3 Hoge, E. A., Bui, E., Marques, L., Metcalf, C. A., Morris, L. K., Robinaugh, D. J., Worthington, J. J., Pollack, M. H. and Simon, N. M., 2013. Randomized controlled trial of mindfulness meditation for generalized anxiety disorder: Effects on anxiety and stress reactivity. *The Journal of Clinical Psychiatry*, 74(8), pp. 786–92.

4 Luders, E., Cherbuin, N. and Kurth, F., 2015. Forever Young (er): Potential age-defying effects of long-term meditation on gray matter atrophy. *Frontiers in Psychology*, p. 1551; Lippelt, D. P., Hommel, B. and Colzato, L. S., 2014. Focused attention, open monitoring and loving kindness meditation: Effects on attention, conflict monitoring, and creativity – A review. *Frontiers in Psychology*, 5, p. 1083; Colzato, L. S., Ozturk, A. and Hommel, B., 2012. Meditate to create: The impact of focused-attention and open-monitoring training on convergent and divergent thinking. *Frontiers in Psychology*, p. 116; Lutz, A., Slagter, H. A., Dunne, J. D. and Davidson, R. J., 2008. Attention regulation and monitoring in meditation. *Trends in Cognitive Sciences*, 12(4), pp. 163–9; Lutz, A., Slagter, H. A., Rawlings, N. B., Francis, A. D., Greischar, L. L. and Davidson, R. J., 2009. Mental training enhances attentional stability: Neural and behavioral evidence. *Journal of Neuroscience*, 29(42), pp. 13418–27; Marciniak, R., Sheardova, K., Čermáková, P., Hudeček, D., Šumec, R. and Hort, J., 2014. Effect of meditation on cognitive functions in context of aging and neurodegenerative diseases. *Frontiers in Behavioral Neuroscience*, 8, p. 17.

5 Blacker, A., 12 Feb. 2019. We know you didn't keep your New Year's resolutions [blog]. Apptopia. Retrieved from https://blog.apptopia.com/we-know-you-didnt-keep-your-new-years-resolutions.

6 JoanDidion, 30 Jun. 2009. Wise words: Joan Didion's commencement address at UC Riverside in 1975. Retrieved from https://joandidion.wordpress.com/2009/06/30/wise-words-didions-commencement-address-at-uc-riverside-in-1975/.

CHAPTER 4: YOUR LEVELS

1 Centers for Disease Control and Prevention, 9 Jun. 2022. Data and statistics on venous thromboembolism. Retrieved from https://www.cdc.gov/ncbddd/dvt/data.html.

2 Ibid.

3 Roser, M., Ortiz-Ospina, E. and Ritchie, H., Oct. 2019. Life expectancy. Our World in Data. Retrieved from https://ourworldindata.org/life-expectancy.

4 Connolly, C., 1938. *Enemies of Promise*. George Routledge & Sons.

5 Abraham, E., Hendler, T., Shapira-Lichter, I., Kanat-Maymon, Y., Zagoory-Sharon, O. and Feldman, R., 2014. Father's brain is sensitive to childcare experiences. *Proceedings of the National Academy of Sciences*, 111(27), pp. 9792–7.

6 Kim, P., Rigo, P., Mayes, L. C., Feldman, R., Leckman, J. F. and Swain, J. E., 2014. Neural plasticity in fathers of human infants. *Social Neuroscience*, 9(5), pp. 522–35.

7 Equality and Human Rights Commission, 6 Jul. 2016. Annual report and accounts 1 April 2015–31 March 2016. Retrieved from https://www.equalityhumanrights.com/sites/default/files/ara_2015-2016.pdf.

8 McKinsey Global Institute, 15 Jul. 2020. COVID-19 and gender equality: Countering the regressive effects. Retrieved from https://www.mckinsey.com/featured-insights/future-of-work/covid-19-and-gender-equality-countering-the-regressive-effects.

9 McKinsey & Company, n.d. Women in the workplace, 2021. Retrieved from https://wiw-report.s3.amazonaws.com/Women_in_the_Workplace_2021.pdf.

CHAPTER 5: BUILDING FOR RESILIENCE

1 Taleb, N. N., 2012. *Antifragile*. Penguin.

2 Schuessler, J., 21 Sep. 2014. Still no flying cars? Debating technology's future. *New York Times*. Retrieved from https://www.nytimes.com/2014/09/22/arts/peter-thiel-and-david-graeber-debate-technologys-future.html.

3 De George, M., 9 May 2022. 'The only thing I saw was a swimmer: Michael Phelps on identity and mental health. *Swimming World*. Retrieved from https://www.swimmingworldmagazine.com/news/the-only-thing-i-saw-was-a-swimmer-michael-phelps-on-identity-and-mental-health/.

4 Goodreads, n.d. Friedrich Nietzsche quotes. Retrieved from https://www.goodreads.com/quotes/137-he-who-has-a-why-to-live-for-can-bear.

5 Burton-Hill, C., n.d. Twixmas bonus episode! How to fail: Clemency Burton-Hill [podcast]. How to Fail with Elizabeth Day. Retrieved from https://podcasts.apple.com/gb/podcast/twixmas-bonus-episode-how-to-fail-clemency-burton-hill/id1407451189?i=1000546170505.

6 Soojung-Kim Pang, A., 2016. *Rest*. Basic Books.

7 Bonos, L., 10 Nov. 2015. Q: Shonda Rhimes, how do you do it all? A: I don't. *Washington Post*. Retrieved from https://www.

washingtonpost.com/news/soloish/wp/2015/11/10/q-shonda-rhimes-how-do-you-do-it-all-a-i-dont/.

8 Topping, A., 12 Sep. 2021. How do UK childcare costs stack up against the best? *Guardian*. Retrieved from https://amp.theguard-ian.com/money/2021/sep/12/how-do-uk-childcare-costs-stack-up-against-the-best.

9 OECD, 2011. The future of families to 2030: A synthesis report. Retrieved from https://www.oecd.org/futures/49093502.pdf.

10 Fry, R., 1 Oct. 2019. The number of people in the average U.S. household is going up for the first time in over 160 years. Pew Research Center. Retrieved from https://www.pewresearch.org/fact-tank/2019/10/01/the-number-of-people-in-the-average-u-s-household-is-going-up-for-the-first-time-in-over-160-years/.

11 Ortiz-Ospina, E. and Roser, M., Feb. 2020. Loneliness and social connections. Our World in Data. Retrieved from https://ourworldin-data.org/social-connections-and-loneliness#loneliness-solitude-and-social-isolation.

12 Insel, T., 2022. *Healing*. Penguin Press.

13 Thaler, R. and Sunstein, C., 2008. *Nudge*. Penguin, p. 8.

CHAPTER 6: WHY QUITTING ISN'T (IMMEDIATELY) THE ANSWER

1 Minkkinen, A. R., 2006. Stay on the bus. The Helsinki bus station theory: Finding your own vision in photography. fotocommunity. Retrieved from http://www.fotocommunity.com/info/Helsinki_Bus_Station_Theory.

2 Meerwijk, E. L. and Weiss, S. J., 2011. Toward a unifying definition of psychological pain. *Journal of Loss and Trauma, 16*(5), pp. 402–12.

3 Liverpool John Moores University, n.d. Universal psychological needs. Retrieved from https://www.ljmu.ac.uk/microsites/promot-ing-healthy-weight-in-pre-school-children/modules/communicat-ing-with-parents/universal-psychological-needs#:~:text=According%20to%20SDT%20there%20are,hunger%2C%20thirst%2C%20sleep.

4 Tolstoy, L., 1980. *Anna Karenina*. Oxford University Press, p. 1.

5 Sons, M. and Niessen, C., 2021. Cross-lagged effects of voluntary job changes and well-being: A continuous time approach. *Journal of Applied Psychology 107*(6).

6 Burkeman, O., 2021. *Four Thousand Weeks*. Bodley Head.

7 Lamont, T., 26 Feb. 2022. Daisy Edgar-Jones on life after Normal

People: 'Should I be living it up more? Is this how our 20s are supposed to be? *Guardian*. Retrieved from https://www.theguardian.com/tv-and-radio/2022/feb/26/daisy-edgar-jones-normal-people-intimacy-coaches?CMP=Share_iOSApp_Other.

8 David, S., 2016. *Emotional Agility*. Penguin Life.

9 *You Magazine*, 12 Dec. 2021. Elizabeth Day: 'I've finally learned to quit'. Retrieved from https://www.you.co.uk/elizabeth-day-ive-finally-learned-to-quit/.

CHAPTER 7: LIVING A RICH AND VARIED LIFE

1 Pencavel, J., Apr. 2014. The productivity of working hours. Institute of Labor Economics. Retrieved from https://ftp.iza.org/dp8129.pdf.

2 Den Heijer, A., 2018. *Nothing You Don't Already Know*. CreateSpace Independent Publishing Platform.

3 Bader Ginsburg, R., 1 Oct. 2016. Ruth Bader Ginsburg's advice for living. *New York Times*. Retrieved from https://www.nytimes.com/2016/10/02/opinion/sunday/ruth-bader-ginsburgs-advice-for-living.html.

4 Stanford Report, 14 Jun. 2005. 'You've got to find what you love,' Jobs says. Stanford News. Retrieved from https://news.stanford.edu/news/2005/june15/jobs-061505.html.

5 Diener, E. and Tay, L., 2017. Chapter 6: A scientific review of the remarkable benefits of happiness for successful and healthy living. In: The Centre for Bhutan Studies and GNH, 2017. *Happiness: Transforming the development landscape*. Retrieved from https://philpapers.org/archive/ADLDOT.pdf#page=95.

6 Wellable Labs, n.d. 2021 Employee wellness industry trends report. Retrieved from https://www.wellablelabs.com/research/employee-wellness-industry-trends-reports/2021.

7 World Health Organization, 28 May 2019. Burn-out an 'occupational phenomenon': International Classification of Diseases. Retrieved from https://www.who.int/news/item/28-05-2019-burn-out-an-occupational-phenomenon-international-classification-of-diseases.

8 McFeely, S. and Wigert, B., 13 Mar. 2019. This fixable problem costs U.S. businesses $1 trillion. Gallup. Retrieved from https://www.gallup.com/workplace/247391/fixable-problem-costs-businesses-trillion.aspx.

9 Cross, R., Pryor, G. and Sylvester, D., Nov.–Dec. 2021. How to succeed quickly in a new role. *Harvard Business Review*. Retrieved from https://hbr.org/2021/11/how-to-succeed-quickly-in-a-new-role.

10 Manne, K., 2019. *Down Girl*. Penguin.

CHAPTER 8: FINDING CAREER FULFILMENT

1 Humanists UK, n.d. Religion and belief: some surveys and statistics. Retrieved from https://humanists.uk/campaigns/religion-and-belief-some-surveys-and-statistics.

2 Jones, J. M., 29 Mar. 2021. U.S. church membership falls below majority for first time. Gallup. Retrieved from https://news.gallup.com/poll/341963/church-membership-falls-below-majority-first-time.aspx.

3 Thompson, D., 24 Feb. 2019. Workism is making Americans miserable. *The Atlantic*. Retrieved from https://www.theatlantic.com/ideas/archive/2019/02/religion-workism-making-americans-miserable/583441.

4 O'Keefe, P. A., Dweck, C. S. and Walton, G. M., 2018. Implicit theories of interest: Finding your passion or developing it? *Psychological Science*, 29(10), pp. 1653–64.

5 Buchanan, D., 7 Dec. 2021. I quit my dream job for my mental health. *Grazia*. Retrieved from https://graziadaily.co.uk/amp/life/real-life/quit-dream-job-mental-health/.

CHAPTER 9: THE TRADES OF LIFE

1 de Botton, A., 2016. *The Course of Love*. Penguin.

2 Williams, S., 9 Aug. 2022. Serena Williams says farewell to tennis on her own terms – and in her own words. As told to Rob Haskell. *Vogue*. Retrieved from https://www.vogue.com/article/serena-williams-retirement-in-her-own-words.

3 *Autosport*, 28 Jul. 2022. Sebastian Vettel's full statement on his retirement from F1. Retrieved from https://www.autosport.com/f1/news/sebastian-vettels-full-statement-on-his-retirement-from-f1/10344480/.

4 Cai, D., 12 Nov. 2021. A good newsletter exit strategy is hard to find. *Vanity Fair*. Retrieved from https://www.vanityfair.com/style/2021/11/11/a-good-newsletter-exit-strategy-is-hard-to-find.

5 Smith, M., Yagan, D., Zidar, O. and Zwick, E., 2019. Capitalists in the twenty-first century. *The Quarterly Journal of Economics*, 134(4), pp. 1675–745.

6 Government Equalities Office and Equality and Human Rights Commission, 16 Jun. 2015. Equality Act 2010: Guidance. Retrieved from https://www.gov.uk/guidance/equality-act-2010-guidance.

7 European Commission, n.d. Non-discrimination: Know your rights. Retrieved from https://ec.europa.eu/info/aid-development-coopera-tion-fundamental-rights/your-rights-eu/know-your-rights/equality/non-discrimination_en.

8 Equality and Human Rights Commission, 5 Apr. 2016. Three in four working mothers say they've experienced pregnancy and maternity discrimination. Retrieved from https://www.equalityhu-manrights.com/en/our-work/news/three-four-working-mothers-say-they've-experienced-pregnancy-and-maternity.

9 Brearley, J., 2022. *The Motherhood Penalty*. Simon & Schuster UK.

10 Ormerod, K., 6 Jan. 2020. Before I get back to work . . . Instagram. Retrieved from https://www.instagram.com/p/B6_JBA1BLz4/?igshid=YmMyMTA2M2Y.

11 Preston, R., 20 Jun. 2022. Macmillan 'profoundly sorry' after report finds racist and ableist discrimination claims 'ignored'. Civil Society. Retrieved from https://www.civilsociety.co.uk/news/macmillan-profoundly-sorry-after-report-finds-racist-and-ableist-discrimination-claims-ignored.html.

12 Ross, M. B., Glennon, B. M., Murciano-Goroff, R., Berkes, E. G., Weinberg, B. A. and Lane, J. I., 2022. Women are credited less in science than men. *Nature*, *608*(7921), pp. 135–45.

13 CMI, 20 Jun. 2022. The Inclusion Illusion: CMI research reveals discrimination in the UK workplace is endemic and is holding back the economy and public services. Retrieved from https://www.managers.org.uk/about-cmi/media-centre/press-office/press-releases/the-inclusion-illusion.

14 Cain Miller, C., 15 May 2019. Work in America is greedy. But it doesn't have to be. *New York Times*. Retrieved from https://www.nytimes.com/2019/05/15/upshot/employers-flexible-work-america.html.

15 Goldin, C., 2021. *Career and Family*. Princeton University Press.

16 Ibid.

17 Ibid.

18 Andrew, A., Bandiera, O., Dias, M. C. and Landais, C., 12 Mar. 2021. The careers and time use of mothers and fathers. Institute for Fiscal Studies. Retrieved from https://ifs.org.uk/publications/15360.

19 Maternity Action, May 2021. Shared drive failure: Why we need to scrap Shared Parental Leave and replace it with a more equitable system of maternity & parental leave. Retrieved from https://maternityaction.org.uk/wp-content/uploads/Shared-Parental-Leave-briefing-May-2021.pdf.

CHAPTER 10: MONEY MATTERS

1 Kahneman, D. and Deaton, A., 2010. High income improves evaluation of life but not emotional well-being. *Proceedings of the National Academy of Sciences*, 107(38), pp. 16489–93.

2 Tongue-tied, 11 Jun. 2015. *Orange is The New Black*. Season three, episode seven.

3 Sanburn, J., 9 Dec. 2010. The top 10 of everything of 2010: 9. $75,000. *Time*. Retrieved from https://content.time.com/time/specials/packages/article/0,28804,2035319_2033798_2033781,00.html.

4 Dunn, E. W., Gilbert, D. T. and Wilson, T. D., 2011. If money doesn't make you happy, then you probably aren't spending it right. *Journal of Consumer Psychology*, 21(2), pp. 115–25.

5 Ibid.

6 Zaninotto, P., Batty, G. D., Stenholm, S., Kawachi, I., Hyde, M., Goldberg, M., Westerlund, H., Vahtera, J. and Head, J., 2020. Socioeconomic inequalities in disability-free life expectancy in older people from England and the United States: A cross-national population-based study. *The Journals of Gerontology: Series A*, 75(5), pp. 906–13.

7 Smeets, P., Whillans, A., Bekkers, R. and Norton, M. I., 2020. Time use and happiness of millionaires: Evidence from the Netherlands. *Social Psychological and Personality Science*, 11(3), pp. 295–307.

8 Ibid.

9 Pew Research Center, 17 Dec. 2015. Parenting in America: 2. Satisfaction, time and support. Retrieved from https://www.pewresearch.org/social-trends/2015/12/17/2-satisfaction-time-and-support/.

10 Deloitte, 2022. Striving for balance, advocating for change. The Deloitte global 2022 GenZ & Milliennial survey. Retrieved from https://www2.deloitte.com/content/dam/Deloitte/global/Documents/deloitte-2022-genz-millennial-survey.pdf.

11 Opportunity Insights, n.d. The American Dream is fading. Retrieved from https://opportunityinsights.org/national_trends/.

12 Maverick, J. B., 16 Aug. 2022. S&P 500 average return. Investopedia. Retrieved from https://www.investopedia.com/ask/answers/042415/what-average-annual-return-sp-500.asp#citation-4.

13 Hazell, A., n.d. Compound interest calculator. The Calculator Site. Retrieved from https://www.thecalculatorsite.com/finance/calculators/compoundinterestcalculator.php.

ENDNOTES

14 Burnette, M., 1 Oct. 2022. Compound interest calculator. NerdWallet. Retrieved from https://www.nerdwallet.com/banking/calculator/compound-interest-calculator.

15 World Economic Forum, Mar. 2021. Global gender gap report 2021. Retrieved from https://www3.weforum.org/docs/WEF_GGGR_2021.pdf.

16 Ibid.

17 Buckley, J. and Price, D., 2021. Pensions and divorce: Exploratory analysis of quantitative data: Report of a MICRA Seedcorn Project supported by the Pensions Policy Institute. University of Manchester, Manchester Institute of Collaborative Research on Ageing.

18 Kliff, S., 19 Feb. 2018. A stunning chart shows the true cause of the gender wage gap. *Vox.* Retrieved from https://www.vox.com/2018/2/19/17018380/gender-wage-gap-childcare-penalty.

19 Money Helper, n.d. Average childcare costs. Retrieved from https://www.moneyhelper.org.uk/en/family-and-care/becoming-a-parent/childcare-costs.

20 Kleven, H., Landais, C. and Søgaard, J. E., Jan. 2018. Children and gender inequality: Evidence from Denmark. Working paper 24219. National Bureau of Economic Research. Retrieved from https://www.henrikkleven.com/uploads/3/7/3/1/37310663/kleven-landais-sogaard_nber-w24219_jan2018.pdf.

21 Andrew, A., Bandiera, O., Dias, M .C. and Landais, C., 12 Mar. 2021. The careers and time use of mothers and fathers. Institute for Fiscal Studies. Retrieved from https://ifs.org.uk/publications/15360.

22 Dias, F. A., Chance, J. and Buchanan, A., 2020. The motherhood penalty and the fatherhood premium in employment during Covid -19: Evidence from the United States. *Research in Social Stratification and Mobility, 69,* p. 100542.

23 Andrew, A., Bandiera, O., Dias, M. C. and Landais, C., 12 Mar. 2021. The careers and time use of mothers and fathers. Institute for Fiscal Studies. Retrieved from https://ifs.org.uk/publications/15360.

24 American Psychological Association, 2014. Girls make higher grades than boys in all school subjects, analysis finds. Retrieved from https://www.apa.org/news/press/releases/2014/04/girls-grades.

25 Elsesser, K., 2 Jul. 2019. There are more college-educated women than men in the workforce, but women still lag behind men in pay. *Forbes.* Retrieved from https://www.forbes.com/sites/kimelsesser/2019/07/02/now-theres-more-college-educated-women-than-men-in-workforce-but-women-still-lag-behind-men-in-pay/.

26 Perry, M. J., 14 Oct. 2021. Women earned the majority of doctoral degrees in 2020 for the 12th straight year and outnumber men in grad school 148 to 100. AEI. Retrieved from https://www.aei.org/carpe-diem/women-earned-the-majority-of-doctoral-degrees-in-2020-for-the-12th-straight-year-and-outnumber-men-in-grad-school-148-to-100/.

27 Kempster, H., Nov. 2018. Gender in the graduate labour market. Prospects Luminate. Retrieved from https://luminate.prospects.ac.uk/gender-in-the-graduate-labour-market.

28 Andrew, A., Bandiera, O., Dias, M. C. and Landais, C., 12 Mar. 2021. The careers and time use of mothers and fathers. Institute for Fiscal Studies. Retrieved from https://ifs.org.uk/publications/15360.

CHAPTER 11: IMPACTFUL WORK

1 Manzoor, S., 10 Jun. 2017. Studs Terkel's Working – new jobs, same need for meaning. *Guardian*. Retrieved from https://www.theguardian.com/books/2017/jun/10/studs-terkel-working-rereading.

2 Plummer, J., 16 Aug. 2017. Women more likely to donate than men, IOF study finds. *ThirdSector*. Retrieved from https://www.thirdsector.co.uk/women-likely-donate-men-iof-study-finds/fundraising/article/1442144.

3 Carers UK, n.d. 10 facts about women and caring in the UK on International Women's Day. Retrieved from https://www.carersuk.org/news-and-campaigns/features/10-facts-about-women-and-caring-in-the-uk-on-international-women-s-day.

4 NCVO, 1 Sep. 2021. UK Civil Society Almanac 2021. Retrieved from https://data.ncvo.org.uk/workforce/.

5 Igielnik, R., 18 Aug. 2020. Men and women in the U.S. continue to differ in voter turnout rate, party identification. Pew Research Center. Retrieved from https://www.pewresearch.org/fact-tank/2020/08/18/men-and-women-in-the-u-s-continue-to-differ-in-voter-turnout-rate-party-identification/.

6 Bani, M. and Giussani, B., 2010. Gender differences in giving blood: A review of the literature. *Blood Transfusion*, 8(4), p. 278.

7 Lippa, R., 1998. Gender-related individual differences and the structure of vocational interests: The importance of the people–things dimension. *Journal of Personality and Social Psychology*, 74(4), pp. 996–1009; Su, R., Rounds, J. and Armstrong, P. I., 2009. Men and things, women and people: A meta-analysis of sex differences in interests. *Psychological Bulletin*, 135(6), pp. 859–84.

8 Snyder, T., 16 Mar. 2018. Vladimir Putin's politics of eternity. *Guardian.* Retrieved from https://www.theguardian.com/news/2018/mar/16/vladimir-putin-russia-politics-of-eternity-timothy-snyder.

9 Martin, G., 2021. *Be The Change.* Sphere.

10 Centre for Effective Altruism, n.d. Retrieved from https://www.effectivealtruism.org/.

11 Centre for Effective Altruism, n.d. What is effective altruism? Retrieved from https://www.effectivealtruism.org/articles/introduction-to-effective-altruism.

12 Gladwell, M., 2008. *Outliers.* Little, Brown and Company.

13 McCarthy, J., 18 Feb. 2016. Happy birthday Toni Morrison – 11 of her quotes to celebrate. Global Citizen. Retrieved from https://www.globalcitizen.org/en/content/10-toni-morrison-quotes-to-celebrate-her-birthda-2/.

14 Giving What We Can, n.d. Retrieved from https://www.givingwhatwecan.org/.

15 Giving What We Can, n.d. Comparing charities: How big is the difference? Retrieved from https://www.givingwhatwecan.org/charity-comparisons?utm_source=gwwc_giving_guide&utm_medium=pdf&utm_campaign=gwwc_giving_guide_2021.

16 Double the Donation, 2022. Corporate giving and matching gift statistics. Retrieved from https://doublethedonation.com/matching-gift-statistics/.

17 The Ezra Klein Show, 31 Aug. 2021. Transcript: Ezra Klein answers listener questions. *New York Times.* Retrieved from https://www.nytimes.com/2021/08/31/podcasts/transcript-ezra-klein-ask-me-anything.html.

18 Zinn, H., 2018. *You Can't be Neutral on a Moving Train.* Beacon Press.

ABOUT THE AUTHOR

Credit: Alexandra Cameron

Rebecca Anderton-Davies is an investment banker, yoga practitioner and sometimes teacher, author, community builder, and mother of two young sons. She is based in London.

She is 15+ years into a successful career as a banker, first as a currency sales-trader, then as a senior relationship manager, and most recently as head of EMEA for a new business within her firm.

Rebecca has built two Instagram communities with a follower count of nearly 300k: her personal account where she shares her unique combination of career, family life, and her yoga self practice, and her yoga community account. She published her first book – The Book of Yoga Self Practice – with Yellow Kite in 2020.

books to help you live a good life

Join the conversation and tell
us how you live a #goodlife

🐦 @yellowkitebooks
f YellowKiteBooks
P Yellow Kite Books
📷 YellowKiteBooks